How to Ride a Winning Dressage Test

How to Ride a Winning Dressage Test

The Judge's Guide to
Step-by-Step Improvement

Major-General Jonathan R. Burton
with Darlene Sordillo

Houghton Mifflin Company / Boston

Library of Congress Cataloging in Publication Data
Burton, Jonathan R.
  How to ride a winning dressage test.
  1. Dressage tests. I. Sordillo, Darlene.
II. Title.
SF309.6.B87   1985   797.2'4   85-66
ISBN 0-395-37530-4
ISBN 0-395-38217-3 (pbk.)

Printed in the United States of America

V 10 9 8 7 6 5 4 3 2

FRONTISPIECE: One of General Burton's students, Anna
Robinson-Fradin, on her horse, Brion.

Contents

Preface

This manual is designed for riders who are, or who plan to be, active dressage competitors. It is not intended as a substitute for regular instruction, but rather as a supplement to it. Even the most experienced rider would have difficulty implementing the guidelines in this book without the benefit of a trained eye on the ground from time to time.

However, since the American Horse Shows Association (AHSA) and the Federation Equestre Internationale (FEI) limit the number of judges they license, not all riders have the opportunity to train under an instructor who is also a certified dressage judge. Hence the merit — and the emphasis — of this book: to give the competitor a "judge's-eye view" of the current AHSA dressage tests. By talking the rider through the movements required in each test, the book should better enable you to improve your scores and to advance through the progressive levels of dressage.

Since this book is geared toward the competitive aspects of dressage, the authors presume a certain level of competence on the rider's part. It would be futile to attempt to follow the directives in this book — or to compete at a dressage show — unless you have already developed a basic balanced seat and are familiar with the principles of dressage. Your own instructor and any of the fine books available on the fundamentals of dressage should thus prepare you to "ride before the judge" in the following pages.

J.R.B

D.S.

August 1984

Acknowledgments

The authors wish to extend their gratitude to the following dressage enthusiasts, who so kindly contributed to the illustrations in this book:

Anna Robinson-Fradin of Terrybrooke Farm, Rehoboth, Massachusetts, one of General Burton's students, who rode her horse, Brion, through many of the test movements photographed.

John and Dianne Pingree, owners of Flying Horse Farm in South Hamilton, Massachusetts, who provided the use of their dressage arenas for the cover photograph.

Sara Johnston, a Boston architect and dressage competitor, who has ridden in General Burton's clinics and who drew the diagrams of the test figures.

Barry Kaplan, a dressage enthusiast and owner of The Finer Image photo labs in Danvers, Massachusetts, who did all the photography for this book.

How to Ride a Winning Dressage Test

1. Training Level

YOUR FIRST DRESSAGE COMPETITION

The Training Level tests provide the horse — and quite often, the rider — with an introduction into formal dressage competition. These tests are, as their name implies, a vehicle for training the relatively green or unschooled horse in the basic movements of dressage. While the tests at this level are not particularly difficult or demanding, the rider may find it a challenge to guide his uninitiated mount through the required paces.

Take heart, however, for the judge takes these factors into consideration. He can recognize a three- or four-year-old horse by its physical development, attitude, and relative lack of balance. Since a horse at this stage has probably been under saddle for only a matter of months, the judge realizes the horse hasn't had a chance to be exposed to showground distractions. Acclimating the young horse to the competitive environment is one of the functions of riding him through the Training Level tests.

While neophyte dressage horse-and-rider teams often make up the bulk of the Training Level entries at any show, the judge will not be surprised to see a few other combinations. Another common one is the inexperienced rider on a high-level horse. Subscribing to the well-documented theory that "good horses make good riders," some instructors advise fledgling dressage enthusiasts to purchase a horse who knows more than they do about dressage. Often a pupil will advance more rapidly on a trained horse, yet he may very well need to spend some time in the Training Level classes until he learns to "push the right buttons" for the higher-level movements. The judge will recognize the disparity between the abilities of the pair because the rider, with a somewhat undeveloped and insecure seat, will look appropriate at Training Level. The horse, on the other hand, is likely to carry himself in a more advanced frame, showing the balance and muscular development that come with progressive dressage training. There is no automatic penalty or bonus for the green rider with a trained dressage horse, but the rider may have some difficulty keeping the horse in the proper frame for Training Level and keeping him from anticipating higher-level movements (such as lengthenings across the diagonal) that are not part of these tests.

Somewhere in the middle of the two extremes comes another category: a fairly competent rider with a horse who was initially trained for another type of riding. The horse, unlike the rider, did not begin his dressage schooling until he had already reached his prime. Perhaps the horse's previous owner took a sudden interest in dressage, or perhaps a trainer along the way noticed some dressage potential in the animal. Whatever the case, many former race horses, hunters, and pleasure horses have been successfully converted to dressage mounts. They begin their competitive dressage careers along with the other novice horses or riders in that great melting-pot of classes, the Training Level tests.

No matter where the horse has come from, the judge will be looking for the same characteristics — a willing, obedient mount who moves forward freely, responding to the rider's aids and accepting the bit. Although the horse at this stage of training is only expected to stretch onto the bit in a relaxed manner, the increasing degree of competence in lower-level dressage riders has resulted in more and more Training Level horses being shown "on the bit." This is not required, but it can favorably impress the judge, so long as the horse is moving from behind and is not being "boxed up" or impeded from moving forward by a rider who is using rein pressure to create a false impression of having the horse on the bit. The judge can easily discern such an attempt and will punish it as severely as he will the horse who evades and comes behind the bit. If your horse has the latter tendency, it is better to leave his mouth alone and to encourage him to move forward in a relaxed Training Level frame, with his nose somewhat ahead of the vertical.

The judge wants to see good, solid basics established in your horse at this level — not complications or attempts to overdo, which will only hinder the horse's progress at the higher levels. The Training Level tests are considered extremely important because they are designed to evaluate the fundamental dressage training the horse has received. The movements required at this level are the building blocks from which the more advanced movements will come. Dressage is like learning a foreign language — if your basic sentence structure is wrong, you will be hopelessly befuddled when it comes time to make compound sentences. So don't fall into the trap of thinking you can fudge a few movements because after all, "it's only Training Level." The judge does not share this shortsighted philosophy.

While the tests at this level were designed not to tax the psyche or the physical abilities of the young horse, they do require a certain degree of training. A horse is not ready to compete at Training Level until he readily responds to the rider's aids. The horse should go forward when you say, turn when you say, and perform simple, one-gait transitions (such as walk-to-halt or trot-to-walk) willingly and obediently. He must also be able to perform the specific schooling figures required in the Training Level tests, such as the 20-meter circle.

Unfortunately, too many riders try to force an unprepared young horse into a Training Level test. The result is a horse who is heavy in front and goes around the arena with his mouth open, pulling and unmanageable. The horse spends more time going sideways than forward, missing more of the required transitions than he achieves. The judge forms a negative impression when a rider enters the arena with a horse he has obviously schooled only three or four times.

Proper preparation for the Training Level tests involves exercises that will teach the horse to move forward with balance and rhythm, developing the precision required to perform the movements of the test. The following is a routine I like to use when schooling a Training Level horse:

Start each session by encouraging the horse to walk freely on a fairly loose rein, which allows him to stretch and to "get the engine warm." After 10 or 15 minutes I make the transition to rising trot, initially working on straight lines to get the horse moving under me, obeying me, and going in balance. Then I'll work on the diagonals, the center line, and the entire arena (which is actually a rectangle) several times, to get the horse going along rhythmically.

Next I like to spend another 10 or 15 minutes working on the turning movements. I usually start with the serpentine because it makes the horse bend continuously and change his bend frequently, while he hopefully keeps his balance, goes forward from behind, remains engaged, and continues to accept the bit. Then I do some half-circles, often working into 10-meter circles, such as those required in First Level Test 3, where you trot down the center line and make a circle at L and I (see p. 67). Eventually I end up making a figure eight at X.

At this point I will let the horse walk briefly on a loose rein to relax him. After working on the free walk, I pick up the working walk to do some turns on the haunches, which is the first lateral movement I introduce. The turn on the haunches is an excellent way to get the horse lighter and more balanced, because he has to move his heavy front end and pivot around his hind end (see photos, p. 119). You'll find that horses pick this up quickly. As the horse's training progresses, I work into leg-yielding at the walk, which is another good suppling and balancing exercise that can be done with Training Level horses. Although the leg-yield is not required until First Level, I think it should be used in schooling as soon as the horse has developed sufficient strength for dressage exercises.

After working through this walk routine, I'll do some transitions from sitting trot to canter, usually on a 20-meter circle. Here I'm looking for smooth transitions, with the horse going from one balanced gait into another without his head coming up. The more difficult transition, of course, is the downward one from canter to trot. The rider must ensure that the horse makes the transition from the rear to the front, by using the seat rather than the reins (the latter, unfortunately, being the common tendency in our country). I'll work on the trot-to-canter-to-trot transitions in both directions, time and time again, for they help build up the horse's strength and improve his balance.

Now we progress to transitions with only a few steps at trot before the canter. This lightens the horse and improves his cadence and balance. As the horse advances in his canter work, you can start to spiral him in and out on a circle. Usually the canter is a trifle long and fast initially. Spiraling in helps the horse's canter become rounder and more balanced, with a higher degree of engagement. I'll often use the leg-yield to spiral in to a 10-meter circle, not allowing the horse to trot, and then spiral back out.

Eventually I'll work the horse using the whole arena, to ensure that he keeps the same tempo on the long side. If he speeds up, I'll go back to circle and work on that until the horse will stay in the same frame on the long side. When he can do that in balance I'll begin to work on some changes of lead. I might ride through the center of the arena, trot at X, and take the other lead. Or I may do canter serpentines of three loops, asking for smooth transitions by using the trot to change the bend.

That works us up to large counter-canters, using the width of the whole arena. I find the counter-canter to be an excellent suppling, balancing, and conditioning exercise, which improves the horse's balance and cadence. But you should not ask a young horse for a counter-canter until he is confirmed in his normal canter and until you have perfected his transitions, serpentines, and 20-meter circles.

Usually I end a session with a green horse by doing some lengthenings, which we did earlier in this session at the free walk. Once I have the canter under control, I'll ask for a lengthening down the long side, being sure I get two transitions — one at the start and one at the finish. I usually do my trot lengthenings after the canter, because I find the horse does them better. Before asking for a trot lengthening, I'll use some form of balancing. The simplest method is to do a 10-meter circle at the sitting trot. In the circle, you collect the horse and cause him to balance himself to make the turn, which puts him in the proper frame to do some extension without moving faster or doing a running trot. I find the Training Level horse's lengthenings quickly improve if they are taken from the 10-meter circle. Later they can be taken from a shoulder-in, and with even more training, the extension can come from a series of half-halts. But at this point, you don't want to overcomplicate matters for the horse or ask him to do movements for which he is not mentally or physically prepared.

You can use segments of this schooling routine when warming the horse up at a competition for a Training Level test, although you may have to make some adjustments to suit your horse's temperament and physical condition. Obviously, a nervous horse should be warmed up differently than a phlegmatic horse. The former needs to be calmed down and relaxed, so he will appear submissive; the latter needs to be invigorated, so he will move forward and show some brilliance. The length of time you spend warming up depends on which type of horse you're showing. I've seen people ride into the arena with anywhere from a few minutes to three hours of warm-up, either of which can be effective, given the varying nature of horses. You have to know your own horse.

As a general guideline, I find it helps prepare a horse for his first test to take him out several hours in advance and work the straight-lines routine previously mentioned, ending with serpentines, turns, and simple transitions. Put the horse back in his stall or trailer until shortly before the test, when you can spend 10 or 15 minutes riding some of the specific movements required in the test, taking care not to do them in the actual sequence or at the location in which they occur in the test. Horses learn very quickly to anticipate, so you're asking for trouble if you ride your horse through the exact test pattern, even when practicing at home. If your horse thinks he should finish every test with a halt on the center line at X (as is required in Training Level Test 1), you'll have problems in the next test (Test 2), which ends with a halt at G instead. The point is that the rider, not the horse, should memorize the test. The judge wants to see that you are clearly in the driver's seat, guiding the horse through each movement.

When the rider before you has finished his test, you may begin your final warm-up around the perimeter of the arena. If the show is running on or ahead of schedule, the judge may have time to notice your warm-up and form some general impressions. Show him you know what you are doing by being workmanlike and taking advantage of your time to introduce your horse to the possibly unfamiliar environs of the dressage arena. This should be done at the trot, so you have time to ride all the way around the arena at least once. Right away, find out if your horse is going to shy from the judge's table or trailer, the dressage letters, or any decorative flowers. It's a good idea to take the horse between the judge's stand and the letter C, because a number of green horses are sure the boogeyman is hiding there. If your horse spooks or snorts, ride him through there several times in both directions. If there is time, you might also do a few trot-to-walk-to-halt transitions, to try to get the horse relaxed yet responsive enough to move between your leg and hand.

Bear in mind that as soon as you enter the arena, I'm going to be judging the ability of the horse to move, the quality of the transitions, and the accuracy of the ride (in that order). So if you lack one of these criteria, you should try to make it up with another. These overall impressions I form of your ride will determine your scores for the "collective marks," which are computed at the end of the test and are added to your final score.

Beyond the collective marks and the specific test movements on which you are judged in dressage tests, there are other considerations that can improve your score. Many of these factors apply at the higher levels as well, but they are of particular value to Training Level riders, who are likely to be less seasoned in a competitive situation. They include:

Errors. If you go off-course or forget a movement in the test, you lose two points for the first error. The judge will signal that you have made an error by blowing the whistle or ringing the bell. If this happens during a test, try to keep your composure. When you become upset, the horse is likely to follow suit. Some riders are so tense that they panic over an error. Normally that reaction only compounds the problem, because the rider's mind may go blank and then the situation rapidly degenerates. An inexperienced rider may be so flustered that he or she finds it difficult — or even impossible — to proceed with the test. Experienced riders, on the other hand, immediately realize their error when they hear the whistle and correct themselves before the judge has to address them. The key here is to rectify the mistake with the least amount of consternation as possible, and then proceed with the test.

Callers. In Europe, and particularly in Germany, the person who calls or reads the test to you is considered extremely important. Those countries have more variety in their tests and more tests at each level, so the caller becomes increasingly necessary. Managers of dressage competitions overseas hire a skilled, professional reader who calls the test for everyone. It is very expertly done and therefore is of value to the rider. In this country, however, we often hear inexperienced readers calling the test. They may be difficult for the rider to hear, or may not give the rider enough warning to prepare for the movements. Even worse, the caller may inadvertently skip a movement or read the test otherwise incorrectly, causing the rider to go off course. If this happens to you, your test score will reflect that error, even though it wasn't your fault.

Often dressage competitions — especially those at Training Level, where riders tend to rely on a caller — are held up for time because the rider panics if his caller isn't there when it is time to enter the arena. The judge may, or may not, condescend to wait for the reader to arrive. It is rude for your reader to be late, for it sets back the timing of the competition. This makes for a longer day for the judge, and everyone else involved.

Overall, I am lukewarm to the idea of having a test called. A reader with an extremely loud voice can be rather disconcerting and disruptive to riders who are trying to ride other tests in nearby arenas. You will find it difficult to concentrate on the test you are riding when a reader in an adjacent arena is announcing a completely different set of movements. If you have a reader as well, his or her voice may mingle with that of the other reader, confusing both you and the rider in the next arena.

It is not good to become dependent on having a caller at this level, because if you advance to the FEI dressage levels or branch out into combined training, a reader is not allowed. I would advise a beginning rider to try to memorize each test thoroughly beforehand, as do the good riders. International dressage veteran Lendon Gray always rides her tests from memory and never makes an error, which can't help but impress the judge. I have seen her ride every test from Training Level to Grand Prix in one day, without a caller. That makes for a tremendous performance, and the judges can't help but take it into consideration. Since you have only a few Training Level tests to memorize, you are probably better off to do so and ride without a caller, unless absolute stage fright precludes it.

Number of tests. Some Training Level riders have the mistaken idea that their day at a competition is wasted unless they ride in five or six classes. I feel that is entirely too much to ask of the horse, who will certainly find it difficult to keep his energy and concentration, and to be obedient and precise in that many tests. If you are taking a green horse to his first or second show, two classes are plenty of exposure and work for him — and probably for you, too.

Frame. The Training Level horse should have a long, relaxed frame and a soft jaw contact with the bit. Although he is not required to be on the bit at this stage of training, more and more horses competing at Training Level are showing a First Level frame, with the head carriage slightly higher and the face closer to the vertical. As long as the horse's steps are coming from behind, most judges will reward this more developed frame.

However, the horse who is so advanced that he executes a Training Level test in a Third Level frame causes quite some controversy among dressage judges. Some say the higher-level frame should not be rewarded because it is not what the test asks for; others say the horse is doing the working gaits more elegantly, with more collection and rhythm, and therefore should be rewarded. However, as a standard the working gaits should be free-flowing and not collected to the extent they are in a Third Level frame, which requires more engagement of the hindquarters and more elevation of the head and neck. Therefore, I personally feel the horse should go in a Training Level frame and that a higher-level frame should not be scored generously.

If your horse has advanced so much in his dressage schooling that he is completely on the bit and moves with balance in a higher and rounder frame than Training Level calls for, perhaps you should consider moving up to First Level. Often, riders begin to achieve success at Training

Level and because they enjoy winning, they stay at that level for long periods of time. I do not feel that is the proper attitude. As the horse progresses in training, he should advance through the higher levels of dressage competition. The rider, if not the trainer, should realize when the horse is moving sufficiently in balance to move up a level. Sometimes, I feel obligated to tell the rider on his or her test sheet that the horse does not belong at the level at which it is being shown. (As a rough guideline, when you are scoring consistently in the 60's, it is probably time to move up. An exceptionally good mover, however, may even score in the 70's at Training Level because the movements are not very difficult for him.)

Turnout. There is, of course, no numerical score given for the dress and appearance of horse and rider, but that doesn't mean you should overlook it. Dressage competitions are very formal, so your attire should reflect that. A rider in a clean black jacket, white breeches, and shiny boots presents a sharp appearance and shows respect for the sport and the judge. Likewise, your horse and tack should be clean. I'm not going to give you points for showing up in an expensive, German-imported, rolled bridle, but I will form a negative impression of you and your horse if your tack is in disrepair.

As soon as the judge spots you, he or she forms an initial impression from the overall picture you present. When I see a rider enter the arena dressed correctly, I subconsciously anticipate that he knows how to ride correctly. The converse is also true: a rider who looks disorganized will probably ride his test that way. Riders with long hair look particularly sloppy if they do not tuck it up into a hairnet. Horses whose manes and tails are not braided (or at least pulled) look unkempt. The point is, you want to make yourself and your horse look as "dressage-y" as possible. If you look like you belong in a dressage arena, you are starting your test one step ahead of the game, so to speak. And in a competitive situation, every little bit helps. If your seat or your horse's gaits are lacking, your turnout becomes even more important in giving you at least a semblance of credibility as a dressage rider.

Whips. It seems that part of the uniform these days is a dressage whip, which I find is normally longer than it needs to be. Some riders — particularly those in California — even warm up with two whips. Several years ago, before the tests were revised, whips were not allowed during a test and were grounds for elimination. Personally, I would like to see the rule allowing whips removed, and that is probably the general consensus among judges. However, while the rule is in effect for Training through Fourth Level (excluding qualifying classes), you cannot penalize a rider for taking advantage of it. Almost all riders carry a whip into the arena now, but 99 percent of the time they never use it, so it just ends up getting in their way. At Training Level, you may have a horse who won't take the canter or who misses the correct lead without a reinforcing tap of the whip. In that case, by all means carry a whip, but show the judge that you know enough to use it when necessary. If, however, you have no intention of using the whip, don't carry one.

Spurs. In my estimation, spurs are a different matter than whips. Once your seat and legs have become secure enough to handle a pair of spurs, they should become part of the uniform, just like your boots and breeches. From that point on, you always wear them. Presumably a rider isn't ready to compete until he has developed an adequate seat, so his legs should be quiet enough for a pair of spurs even at Training Level. It's sort of the idea that you "earn" your spurs. Once your instructor tells you to buy spurs, you keep them on whenever you ride. So I like to see a rider from Training Level on wear spurs, which are required in the FEI levels.

Timing. Dressage tests are scheduled to the minute for each test ride. Although you are not required to ride your test before your scheduled time, you may be asked to do so if a rider before you scratches. In this case, you have the option of riding your test earlier than you had expected, or you may decline and use all the time allotted you for schooling. I prefer riders to show courtesy to the show management and the judge by being prepared to ride a few minutes early if necessary.

The judge will not "hold it against you" if you do insist on waiting until your scheduled time, but if it has been a long day, he is bound to be irritated if he has to sit idle for 10 minutes while you continue to warm up. As a result of your lengthy schooling time, the judge will expect a solid performance and will be sure to give you the full brunt of his critique when you ride before him. If you have used the extra time well and ride an exceptional test, it won't matter. But if you school for an extra 10 minutes and then ride a mediocre test, your scores will most certainly reflect that, with little benefit of doubt from the judge. In the higher levels he may be more understanding, but the movements at Training Level are so basic that they do not require an extensive or lengthy warm-up.

Now you are ready for me to "judge" you in an imaginary dressage competition, breaking down the test piece by piece. As I talk you through each segment of the test, you should become more aware of how the judge arrives at a score for each set of movements grouped under a certain number on the test sheet. By improving your performance movement-by-movement, your overall percentage score for the test is bound to increase.

AHSA TRAINING LEVEL TEST 1

[1]

A Enter working trot rising
X Halt. Salute. Proceed working trot rising
C Track to the right

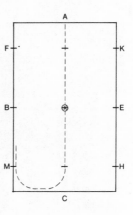

Since the entrance and the first set of movements set the tone for your entire test, give yourself a bonus by entering from the horse's "good" side. Keeping in mind that most horses are somewhat stiff to one side, you should finish your final warm-up around the arena on your horse's good side, so he can make a smoother and more balanced entrance.

Probably the most important movement contributing to your first score is the entrance to the halt. In the current Training Level tests, you have the option of going from the trot to the walk to the halt, or directly from the trot to the halt, the latter being more difficult. I think the rider should take advantage here and use a few steps of walk before the halt. Some riders feel they can impress the judge by coming directly to the halt; this is true only if it is executed smoothly. I would much rather see a few walk steps and the horse stay in balance for the halt than to see an abrupt transition from trot to halt which causes the horse to toss his head up. Since the judge is sitting at C, directly facing you on the center line, he or she has a clear view of the position of the horse's head throughout this initial movement. The steadier it stays, the better.

Sometimes a Training Level horse will move behind when he is at the halt. This is as serious an error as head-tossing and must be scored down. The judge wants to see the horse enter the arena absolutely straight, then make the halt transition smoothly from rear to front, with a few balanced walk steps in between. Keep your legs on the horses's sides so he won't wobble at the walk and fall into a sloppy halt. Lighten the horse beforehand and prepare him for the transition with a few half-halts as he approaches X, using your back and seat — not just your hands — to drive the horse down to the halt. The judge doesn't necessarily expect a horse to halt absolutely square at Training Level, but he would like to see the front legs square and the horse standing straight on the center line, without leaning to the side or fidgeting.

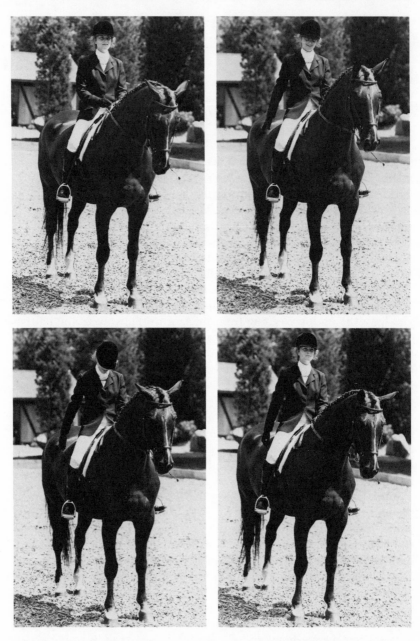

The proper halt-and-salute sequence on the center line at X. First make a square halt at X and establish eye contact with the judge. Drop your hand, nod your head, raise your head, then return your hand to the rein, as in the first picture.

Once you have made the halt, the horse should stand still while you make a dramatic salute. Make sure you take the reins in one hand as you salute. Some nervous riders keep the reins in both hands during the salute, but this will cost you two points for an error. I like to see the salute done with a flourish, which you can accomplish by using this four-step process (see photos): drop your right hand (the left is permissible if it makes you more comfortable) to your side; bow your head slightly; raise your head in the same manner; and take the rein back into your hand. A man should hold his hat in the hand he drops for the salute. Since the salute is a greeting to the judge, it is courteous to make eye contact and show a pleasant facial expression during it.

If your horse objects to standing still for the salute and begins to walk in the middle of it, finish your salute quickly and move on down the center line toward the judge. You won't gain points by fighting with the horse for another halt. Try to make it look as though you planned for the horse to walk on by calmly going with him and proceeding with the test.

Squeeze the horse gently with your legs and use your seat to urge him into a trot toward the judge at C. Since a great deal of this test is precision, you can improve your score by staying straight on the center line until you approach the end of the arena. You can further impress the judge by riding clear down to the end, for a great number of Training Level riders begin to make their turn too soon. The judge wants to see an easy, balanced turn at C, with the same bend you would use for a 10-meter circle. Straighten the horse out on the short side and then use your inner leg to guide him into the corner, bending him on the same arc as a 10-meter circle so he won't "fall in" or "pop a shoulder." That way, you are effectively using this movement to show the judge how much obedience and precision you have instilled in your Training Level horse.

[2]

B Circle right 20 meters
B Working trot sitting

The 20-meter circle should be what it says — 20 meters across and a circle. Here is where the precision comes in. The judge looks for a true circle, but more often than not he sees the rider make an egg-shaped figure, usually with the second half shorter than the first half. It is difficult for lower-level riders to maintain a rhythmical, complete circle unless they have done their homework. It takes quite some practice to learn how to describe a perfect circle when you're on a horse's back. I often find it useful in a schooling situation to take a 10-meter string and hold it 10 meters in from C, drawing a 20-meter circle on the arena to show people where it goes. The circle goes clear out to the edge of the arena and if you're riding in a small (20m x 40m) arena, which is the size used for the Training Level tests at most competitions, the 20-meter circle at B comes a full 10 meters from X, or midway between X and C (see diagram of small arena, p. 206).

While the judge is assessing the accuracy of your circle, he is at the same time observing whether your horse is rhythmical, in balance, and is bent to the inside. If he bends to the outside and pops a shoulder, as often happens when the rider can't get the horse over to B, that is scored as insufficient (no better than a 4).

When you follow the circle back to B, the judge is looking for you to change from a rising trot to a sitting trot, with no change in the rhythm of the horse's gait nor the head carriage. Since many Training Level riders have less-than-confirmed seats, when they go from rising to sitting trot they often bounce and jar the horse's mouth. That causes the horse's head to come up and his gait to change. Some riders, in an attempt to avoid this, will hang on the horse's mouth and slow him down because they find they bounce less at a slower tempo. The judge can see through this and will penalize you accordingly as insufficient. Unfortunately, there are no schooling tips I can give you to correct the situation, except to work on your seat until you achieve enough relaxation in your pelvis and enough strength in your seat so that your hands are not jarred by the rigidity of your seat and body. Obviously, the rider with a more advanced seat will be better able to keep his horse together through this movement and will score higher in this portion of the test, as he probably will throughout it.

[3]

Between F & A Working canter, right lead

Here the judge wants to see the horse flow from trot to canter, with his head bent to the inside. The rider has more than adequate time to prepare and ask for the upward transition, because this test is rather generous in allowing the rider to ask for the canter at any point between F and A. However, the rider should not be overconfident here. Since many Training Level horses are not immediately responsive to the aids, it may take a few strides before the horse acts on your cue to canter. (Any schooling you've done at home on trot-to-canter and canter-to-trot transitions will pay off here.) Don't wait until the last minute to ask for the canter, when you are nearing A, or you may inadvertently rush the horse into an unbalanced, running gait.

Start giving the canter aid as your body comes parallel to F, at the beginning of the turn in the corner. Since the horse should have already begun to bend into the turn, you are more assured of getting a correct inside lead. (Should you get the wrong lead, bring the horse back to the trot and ask more strongly for the correct lead. Do not let him complete the circle on the wrong lead.) This upward transition from trot to canter is one of the easier movements of this test, provided you can keep your horse between your hand and leg. The judge doesn't want to see your horse lurch forward into the canter, tossing his head. Instead, the picture should be balanced, smooth, and flowing.

[4]

E   **Circle right 20 meters**
Between E & H **Working trot rising**

The movement actually starts at A, where the canter must already have been developed. As you move off from A and begin the turn toward K on the long side, be sure to have the horse properly bent and ride into the corner. Too many Training Level horses take overly generous corners. A balanced horse who is on the aids will ride into the corner as if it were a 10-meter circle. The judge wants to see the horse bent in the corners and on circles, but perfectly straight when he is parallel to the sides of the arena. Sitting atop the horse, be sure you see a difference in the bend of the horse's head and neck during this movement when you go from the corner to the long side and then onto the circle at E.

In this 20-meter canter circle, the judge is looking for the same things he wanted to see in your previous circle at the trot — an accurate circle of the correct size and shape, with the horse properly balanced and maintaining impulsion. He doesn't want to see a horse laboring awkwardly around the circle, with his head bent to the outside.

Prepare at the end of the circle for the next transition, which is to the rising trot, between E and H. The downward transitions are the more difficult ones, particularly for a rider with an insecure seat. Common faults in the canter-to-trot transition occur when the horse throws his head in the air, takes irregular steps, comes off the track, or runs into the trot. The judge wants to see the horse come into your hands as you half-halt him to prepare for the transition. During and after the transition, the horse should remain relaxed, light in your hands, and as close to on the bit as possible.

[5]

C–M–E–K Working walk

In order to ride this movement well, the rider must get the horse balanced as soon as he has made the transition to the trot. This prepares the horse for the next transition down to the walk at C. As you round the turn at H, use that corner to bend the horse. Cheating on the corner gets you nowhere; in fact, it robs you of the opportunity to balance the horse and will cost you a few points. As you approach C, go from the rising trot to the sitting trot for a few steps before asking for the walk. Just before C, half-halt the horse with your outside rein and then drive him with your seat into a walk. He should go immediately into a relaxed, four-beat walk.

At C you are the nearest you will come to the judge at any point in this test, so he or she will take advantage of this opportunity to assess you and the horse at close range. It's easy to spot irregular steps or pacing at the walk here, as well as any tenseness in horse or rider.

From C you should ride into the corner and then straighten out the horse on the long side until he reaches M, where you will turn across the "short diagonal" and head for E. Some horses will shorten their stride as you make the turn; a good judge will pick that up and mark you down for it. The judge at this point is also going to observe how relaxed the horse is and the extent of his overstep in the walk. In the working walk, the horse's hind feet should overstep the front by two to four inches, in a marching, four-beat tempo. As always, the horse should remain relaxed and in balance, accepting the bit.

The rider can gain points here if he knows how to help the horse. To get a good walk, the rider's seat should be secure and the leg aids should alternate: Squeeze with your right leg as the right shoulder comes backward, and with your left leg as the left shoulder comes backward. This encourages the horse to stretch his walk by engaging his hindquarters and overstepping with his hind legs. At the walk, you ride the horse like a bicycle but you have to treat each horse differently. If you squeeze too hard on the sides of a nervous horse, he may scoot forward into the trot unless your seat and hands tell him to stay in the walk. It's a rather delicate balance, one that is achieved by hours of practice and plainly getting to know your horse.

[6]

K Working trot rising
B Circle left 20 meters
B Working trot sitting

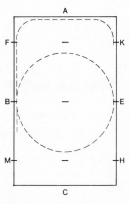

At this point you are a long way from the judge. You should keep the horse parallel to the long side of the arena from E to K, make the transition to trot while the horse is straight, and then ride into the corner. Too many Training Level riders make the transition on the turn back onto the track at E, which is too soon. The judge reads this as sloppiness and a lack of precision. The rider's body will probably block the horse's head from the judge's line of view, so he or she may not be able to see whether the horse's head remains in position as he makes the transition. However, the judge will be able to see whether the horse goes from the walk to the trot flowingly and in the proper rhythm.

Your next task is the 20-meter circle at B (see diagram). Here, the same factors apply as we discussed in the second set of movements in this test (p. 14). Be sure to ride the corner beforehand and start the circle after your body passes the letter B. The judge is looking for precision and accuracy, so spot your circle ahead of time. If the test is in a small arena, your 20-meter circle should come midway between the X–C line, bisecting the B–E line. As you complete the circle, settle back into a smooth sitting trot at B, without disrupting the horse's flow and tempo.

[7]

Between M & C Working canter, left lead

From B, you ride into the next corner and ask for a transition to canter as you begin to make the turn. The judge is looking for a nice, steady, three-beat canter, with the same qualities we discussed in movement #3 of this test. (Since dressage horses are meant to be supple on both sides, any movement you ride in one direction should be repeated on the other hand. The tests reflect this philosophy, so my directives for movements toward the end may be brief, to avoid repetition, unless the movements occur in a different sequence.)

[8]

E   **Circle left 20 meters**
Between E & K   **Working trot rising**

This is a pure repetition — on the opposite rein — of movement #4 in this test. Refer to the directives there.

[9]

A Down center line
X Halt. Salute.

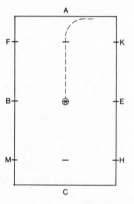

Before you make the turn down the center line at A, you should have prepared for it by what I like to call "organizing your space." You have to use the corner to set up the turn onto the center line (see diagram). So many riders overshoot the center line, barrel out, and then angle back to the center line. This of course shows a serious lack of the precision the judge expects here. The rider needs to have the horse in balance in order to control the turn onto the center line.

As you approach X and prepare for the halt, bear in mind the factors we discussed during your entrance into the arena. The judge wants to see you ride a straight line from A to X, then make a smooth transition to the walk and finally to the halt. Since the judge is sitting straight in front of you at C, he or she has a clear view of you. Keep your legs on the horse's sides to support him and to keep him from wobbling down the center line, as you prepare him for the halt at X with gentle half-halts.

I like to see the rider make a little ceremony out of the halt and salute, executing the movement with precision, so there is somewhat of a show to it. You will be directly in front of me, so establish eye contact and give me a polite smile. After all, you are in a competitive

As viewed from the side, a halt that is not square behind. If it were square, you would see only one hind leg, as is the case in front.

situation, so a little showmanship adds a nice finishing touch to your ride. It also reinforces my overall impression of your test and my opinion of you as a rider.

Under the 1983 revised tests, the judging stops as soon as you salute. Since the judge is probably pressed for time, due to the large numbers of entries at Training Level, he or she begins dictating his general impressions the minute you finish your salute. However, if I have time to watch your exit from the arena, I'll look for you to let the reins slide through your fingers so you have just weight-of-the-rein contact with the horse's mouth. The horse should leave the arena at A in a free, relaxed walk, although he is no longer officially being scored. Often when the horse is on his way out, I see the beautiful, relaxed walk I wish I had seen during the test, when your score would have received the benefit.

Some riders, before they leave the arena, like to make a little circle at A. It may be done for showmanship, but it actually has a more practical function — it keeps the horse from getting the idea that he can duck out of the arena at A. I can't give a rider any specific points for this, but it does add to my general impressions of you as a thinking rider.

AHSA TRAINING LEVEL TEST 2

[1]

A Enter working trot rising
X Halt. Salute. Proceed working trot rising
C Track to the left

As you enter the arena in the rising trot, guide the horse down the center line and look straight ahead at the judge. Here the horse is not "on the bit," but he is accepting it, which is sufficient for Training Level.

The rider should guide the horse around the arena in the rising trot for his warm-up, because most of the movements in this test — including the entrance — are done at the rising trot. When the judge sounds the bell or whistle for you to begin the test, organize yourself so your entrance at A will be as straight as possible. It may help to observe other riders before your test so you can see where the best approach to A is. This is important because once you enter the arena, the judge is looking to see whether your horse is absolutely straight coming down the center line. Keep your eyes straight ahead and spot where you plan to halt at X. If you look down or to the side, you'll throw the horse off balance and probably cause him to drift off the center line.

As we did in the previous test, use the walk for your transition from rising trot to halt, because it makes it easier to keep the horse straight. When you have the halt, put some effort into making your salute formal. Adjust your reins and seat before proceeding down the center line. When you do move out toward the judge, be careful to maintain the straightness you established in your entry. Balance the horse between your legs, keeping the pressure even on both sides, and squeeze him gently into a few steps of walk and then into the trot. Move him straight toward the judge at C.

With a green horse, this may be easier said than done. Many Training Level horses are (or pretend to be) terrified of the judge or trailer, so they may be hesitant to proceed down the center line at this point. You have to ride the horse through this. Make a quick assessment: is my horse genuinely afraid, or is he just spooking as an evasion? In the former case, you need to coax him through it; in the latter, you should exert some stronger persuasion (perhaps the spurs or the whip, if you can be subtle about it). Whatever the situation, correct the problem as quickly and unobtrusively as possible, and then get on with the rest of the test. Your effectiveness in handling such problems bears weight on the judge's general impression of your ride. Use a situation like this to show him you are a rider, not a passenger, as you actively encourage the horse to move down the center line.

As you approach C and make the turn to the left, the judge is only a few meters away from you. He is looking to see if the turning aids are applied, if the horse is bent to the inside, and if the horse goes clear up to the track and makes the turn as though he were on a 10-meter circle.

When you make the turns to get to the long side (H–E–K), the horse should be moving smoothly and should be properly bent to the inside, and the rider should be rising on the correct diagonal. If you can't feel the horse's outside shoulder come forward when you're preparing to take the rising trot, glance down quickly. If for some reason you end up rising on the wrong diagonal, don't change it, or you're likely to disrupt and unbalance the horse. Instead, proceed as you are and try for the correct diagonal when the movement is repeated on the other hand later in the test.

[2]

A Circle left 20 meters
B Working trot sitting

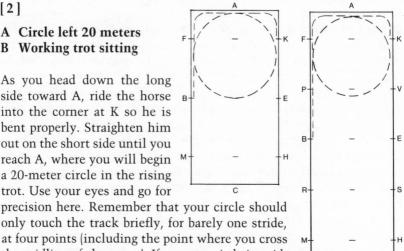

As you head down the long side toward A, ride the horse into the corner at K so he is bent properly. Straighten him out on the short side until you reach A, where you will begin a 20-meter circle in the rising trot. Use your eyes and go for precision here. Remember that your circle should only touch the track briefly, for barely one stride, at four points (including the point where you cross the midline of the arena). If your test is being ridden in a small arena, the 20-meter circle is fairly easy to spot, because it uses half of the arena and comes to X (see diagram at left). In a large arena, the circle comes two meters beyond the V–P line (see diagram at right). In either arena, the judge has a clear view of the size and shape of your circle. A good rider will impress the judge by riding an accurate 20-meter circle, and then following through by not continuing on the circle when he has returned to A. At that point, you should straighten the horse out and then ride into the next corner.

A few strides before B, prepare to make a transition to the sitting trot. Bear in mind that this is a transition for the rider, not the horse. The working trot rising and the working trot sitting are the same gait, so the judge should see no change in the horse's tempo or rhythm when the rider makes the transition from rising to sitting. Often a Training Level rider with an insecure seat will purposely slow the horse down in order to make a smoother transition to sitting trot, but the judge will score the rider down accordingly.

[3]

Between M & C Working canter, left lead

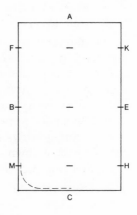

You develop the canter on the turn after M (see diagram), asking the horse to flow from the trot into the upward transition. You should help the horse make the transition and take the proper lead by bending the horse's head to the inside, just enough so you can see the bulge of the inner eyeball. Your outside leg will be slightly behind the girth and your inner leg active and deep on the horse's side (see photo).

The test allows you to pick up the canter between M and C, but ask for it as soon as you pass the first letter, especially if your horse has trouble taking the left lead.

[4]

C Circle left 20 meters
E Working trot sitting

This set of movements repeats those in movement #2 of this test, so the same principles and instructions apply. This time, however, you are at the other end of the arena, directly in front of the judge. He wants to see you initiate the 20-meter circle immediately when you reach C.

When you finish the circle, again ride into the corner as you approach the long side. Although riding into the corners is an excellent way to gain points for precision, very few riders actually bother to do it. A good rider takes advantage of this opportunity to show the judge he knows the difference between riding a circle and a corner, and that he and the horse have the flexibility to execute them both.

The transition from canter to trot at E, like any downward transition, is fairly difficult to achieve with a degree of smoothness. Unfortunately, many Training Level riders pull the horse down into the trot with the reins instead of driving him into it. More often than not, the horse's head will come up and he will go into a rather strong trot, unbalanced and heavy on his front end. The judge wants to see the opposite picture — a flowing downward transition achieved mainly through the rider's seat. Continue down the long side in the trot and ride into the corner right after K to prepare for the next movement, which calls for another downward transition.

[5]

A   Working walk
F–E Free walk on a long rein
E   Working walk

Here the judge wants to see another smooth transition to the working walk. Prepare for it with half-halts after you round the corner from K. Bend the horse into his next turn, using the corner just before F to set up a straight approach across the short diagonal toward E (see diagram). You should be able to show a clear transition from the working walk to the free walk, letting the reins slide through your fingers to encourage the horse to reach out and down with his head and to stretch and lengthen his stride. Since the horse is presented sideways to the judge at this point, he or she can readily measure how free and how long this walk is. Be careful here not to "throw the horse away" by putting him on a loose rein (see bottom photo), which is less contact than the test calls for. The loose rein, sometimes referred to as "riding the horse on the buckle," is not called for until later tests.

Begin to take back the rein contact slightly before E, so you won't suddenly jar the horse's mouth. When you reach E, you should be organized enough to show the judge another transition back to the working walk. Almost invariably, Training Level riders mistakenly think they can take a breather here and do not take advantage of the walk transitions to distinguish one gait from another. These transitions, however, are very important because they show the precision and the training of the horse, which are the objectives of the test.

A good stride in the working walk from A to F (first photo). At F, turn and cross the short diagonal, showing a free walk on a long rein (second photo). Don't let the horse have so much slack that the rein becomes a loose rein, as in the last picture.

[6]

H Working trot rising
C Circle right 20 meters
B Working trot sitting

The next figure is the 20-meter circle, but first you must make a transition at H from the working walk to the rising trot. Usually the upward transitions are fairly balanced and ride relatively well. But to keep the horse precise and in balance, be sure to ride the corner and don't start the 20-meter circle until you reach C.

Ride the circle as we have discussed previously, making it round and accurate, so that it comes either all the way to X (if you are in a small arena), or two meters beyond the R–S line (if you are in a large arena). When you finish the circle, ride into the next corner so you show a difference between the horse's bend on the circle, his straightness on the short side, and his sharper bend on the corner.

On the long side of the arena, go straight ahead to B, where you will try for a smooth transition to the sitting trot. Too many riders use the reins to assist them with their seat, and of course the horse resists by raising his head. The only way to avoid this is to practice your seat at home, preferably on the longe line and under the direction of a skilled dressage instructor.

[7]

Between F & A Working canter, right lead

Before you reach F, prepare the horse for the upward transition with half-halts on the outside rein. He should lightly go into a nice three-beat canter, without raising his head. This repeats movement #3 of this test, but on the opposite rein. So if your horse is stiff to the left, you can probably show the judge a better canter circle here on the right lead.

[8]

A Circle right 20 meters
E Working trot rising

You have already executed this movement — the 20-meter canter circle followed by a transition to the working trot — three times in this test.

However, this time you go from canter to rising trot instead of sitting trot, which will be to your advantage if you have a less-than-secure seat. The same directives apply as we mentioned in movements #2, #4, and #6 of this test.

[9]

MXK Across diagonal

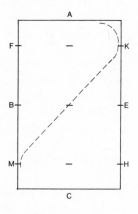

This is the first time the Training Level tests ask you to cross the full diagonal (see diagram). Here it is done at the rising trot. Since you are near the end of the test, the horse may be a bit tired and may not want to show the brilliance he should across the diagonal. We're not asking him to lengthen yet, but the judge does want to see him move with impulsion. Keep your legs on the horse's sides, and direct him in a straight line from M to K.

[10]

A Down center line
G Halt. Salute.

The same considerations apply as in the final movement of the previous test, except this time the halt comes at G. Sight G (halfway between M and H) well beforehand and keep your legs on the horse so he isn't tempted to stop at X. Since this halt places you only six meters away from the judge, establishing eye contact and a polite "thank you" expression on your part are even more important than before.

AHSA TRAINING LEVEL TEST 3

[1]

A Enter working trot sitting
X Halt. Salute. Proceed working trot sitting
C Track to the right

As in most of the AHSA dressage tests, this test is somewhat more difficult than the previous ones at this level because it adds some movements and the transitions occur closer together. In the first two Training Level tests, most of the trot work was done rising. This test, however, is ridden mainly in the sitting trot, so it requires a more secure seat in the rider. And since this test requires you to enter at the sitting trot, your final warm-up around the arena should be at that gait.

The same considerations apply as in our previous entrances, with a few steps of walk between the trot and the halt at X. When you salute, be sure to drop one hand from the reins; otherwise, the judge will mark you down for an error. After the salute, ride clear up to the end of the arena and make proper turns at C and in the corner at M as you head for the long side.

[2]

B Circle right 20 meters

Again, make this a true circle, with the horse in cadence, rhythm, and balance, and bent to the inside. The judge sees a lot more egg-shaped circles here than in the previous Training Level test because the rider doesn't have the end of the arena to guide him. When a test calls for a 20-meter circle in the middle of the arena, as this one does, riders find it considerably more difficult to accurately gauge its dimensions. You want to bisect the B–E line, coming 10 meters to either side of it when you're on the center line and touching the track only at B and E. Riders tend instead to go straight for a few strides along the two long sides of the arena, making in effect a "square" circle. You should come just tangent to the side of the arena for one stride, then immediately curve off the track because the horse is continuously bent on the circle. The 20-meter circle is a precision exercise. In this test, the circle comes close enough to C so that the judge has a clear view of you. It therefore behooves the rider to be very accurate in executing this movement.

[3]

F Working canter, right lead

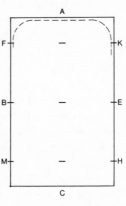

This is one of the movements that makes this test a little more difficult than the previous two at this level. Tests 1 and 2 allowed the rider to develop the upward transition to canter after passing F, or at any point between F and A. This third test requires the canter exactly at F — not before, not after. As the rider's body goes by the letter, the horse should be making the transition. Be sure to ride into the corners here, at F and K (see diagram), for that helps set the horse up for the next movement.

[4]

E Circle right 20 meters
H Working trot sitting

Again, this is a circle in the middle of the arena, so it should bisect the B–E line, as did our previous 20-meter circle in this test. However, this circle is ridden at the canter, followed by a transition to the sitting trot at H, where you are very close to the judge. The downward transition to trot should not occur as the horse is turning in the corner, but rather at H, which is six meters in from the corner. Then you should ride the corner properly, by starting the bend after you've made the transition. The downward transition is really the key here, and the judge is looking to see that the horse does not take irregular steps or bring his head up when going from the canter to the trot.

[5]

C Working walk
MXK Free walk on a long rein
K Working walk

Here, in the middle of the test, we begin to see why the overall series of movements is more difficult than in previous tests. You have just gone from the canter at E to the trot at H, and now you are asked for the working walk at C — three successive downward transitions in a row, all within a relatively short amount of time and space. A responsive, well-schooled horse will benefit here; his antithesis will have difficulty making a good score. Training Level riders often make the walk transition late, after they have passed C, because their horse is perhaps not yet obedient enough to handle the fairly sudden transition. The judge realizes this is not a simple task, so he or she will reward an impressively smooth and balanced transition here. If your horse takes irregular steps, becomes tense, or stays in the trot, however, you can lose a significant number of points quickly in this movement.

Then you cross the long diagonal at the free walk on a long rein. Since we've moved a bit beyond the initial phrase of dressage schooling, you find the horses are often more tense and the riders are worried about them jigging. To keep the horse from breaking into the trot, the rider may incorrectly hang on the reins, which makes the horse even more tense and shortens the walk. When you're on a diagonal like this, moving away from the judge, he can only observe the horse's overstep until you reach X. After that, he can't see the horse at the proper angle to judge his gait. So you have to show the free walk on a long rein almost immediately as you make the turn at M and start across the diagonal.

The judge will be looking for an obvious transition at K to the working walk, in which the horse's stride should become a little higher and shorter as he comes onto the bit or at least closer to it. Unfortunately, when I am judging I rarely see a proper transition made here. You can stand out among the other competitors in the class and gain points by showing me a correct transition from the free walk to the working walk.

[6]

A Halt. Proceed working walk

This movement calls for a downward transition from the working walk to the halt, but it doesn't specify how long the halt should be held. If the halt is relaxed and you feel the horse is square, you might as well sit there a few extra seconds and enjoy it, giving the judge time to take note of your performance. Since the judge has a side view of you from his seat at C, in most cases he can see whether the

horse is square. Most often, we find the front legs square but not the hind (see photo, p. 19). If your horse's halt here is unbalanced and faltering, you might as well move off into the working walk because you have already lost the points for an insufficient halt.

We have a tendency in this country not to spend enough time practicing the halt. You see riders schooling constantly at the walk, trot, and canter, but rarely do they work at transitions to the halt. In Europe they work on the halt transition a great deal, so that every time a halt occurs, it's like a horse going into gear. Every leg goes to a corner and is planted there, which is how the halt should be executed. From the halt, your transition to the walk should be balanced as you move out.

[7]

F Working trot sitting
B Circle left 20 meters

As you leave A, make your turn deep into the corner (see diagram above) so the horse will be straight when you ask for the transition to working trot at F. Almost invariably, riders ask for the trot while they are still on the turn. This is not precise, because they should have finished the turn and started the sitting trot transition at F (see photo). The horse should be straight from that point until he reaches B, where you begin a 20-meter circle at the trot. The same directives apply here as for our previous 20-meter circles.

This horse is showing a good stride in the working trot, which was established at F. The rider is looking ahead to B, where she will begin a 20-meter circle.

[8]

M Working canter, left lead
E Circle left 20 meters

The horse should make the canter transition on the long side at M, while he is straight, and then begin the turn in the corner. A good rider will see an opportunity here to show the judge how precise and how well-trained his horse is by riding the movement correctly. Unfortunately, I see most horses here leaning to the inside and starting the turn when they take the canter. Their scores must reflect this lack of precision.

Go for more precision in your 20-meter circle at E. Since both the large and the small arenas are 20 meters wide, you should ride clear out to the other side of the arena at B — but don't go so far as to make your circle a square — and come back to the track at E.

[9]

K Working trot sitting

With a young horse who is heavy in front, the downward transition from canter to trot is normally a difficult one. Too often, it is done with the reins, causing a few irregular steps until the horse settles into a balanced trot. Movement #9 is scored on whether the horse makes his transition at the letter and on how quickly you can balance him afterwards. Take care to make your next turn after you have made the transition.

[10]

FXH Working trot rising
H   Working trot sitting

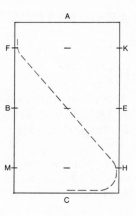

The judge will be looking for the transition from the sitting trot across the short side to the rising trot across the diagonal. Your diagonal line across the arena should be straight (see diagram), and the horse should be balanced, cadenced, relaxed, and rhythmical. As your body comes to H, you make another transition back to the sitting trot.

[11]

MXK Change rein

After you ride along the short side of the arena in front of the judge, you immediately cross the diagonal again, this time from M to K. These are not lengthenings, just ordinary working trots. Horses that have been schooling at First Level will often try to lengthen or extend the trot across the diagonal, but at this point that is not called for. When you reach K, give the horse the proper bend and ride into the corner so he will have a smooth approach toward the center line.

[12]

A Down center line
X Halt. Salute.

This halt is at X, instead of at G as in our previous test. The same considerations apply as were discussed in the final movement of Training Level Test 1.

AHSA TRAINING LEVEL TEST 4

[1]

A Enter working trot sitting
X Halt. Salute. Proceed working trot sitting
C Track to the left

Here your entrance is at the sitting trot, as in the previous test. A green rider with an insecure seat may have problems here with the horse's head going up, but again, that is a direct function of the amount of time you have spent working on your position under the eye of a trained instructor. What you lack in seat development, however, you may compensate for somewhat by riding precise figures. The judge is directly ahead of you at this point, and he is looking for straightness and accuracy on the A–C line. For the balance of this movement, our directives for the entrance in the previous test apply.

[2]

E Turn left
X Circle left 20 meters

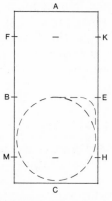

This movement is somewhat different and more difficult. You need to make a turn at E as though you were on a 10-meter circle, but then straighten the horse as you head toward X (see diagram). Start the turn slightly before you reach E, so you will end up on the E–B line. If you wait until you are at E to start the turn, you will overshoot that line and will have to snake back toward it. The judge doesn't want to see your horse make a line like a worm here.

When you come to X, in the center of the arena, you begin a 20-meter circle (see photo). If your test is in a small arena, the circle comes tangent to the sides of the arena and clear up to C, as shown in the diagram. It is considerably more difficult to gauge the dimensions of this circle in a large arena. Since B and R are 12 meters apart, you have to ride two meters inside the R–S line for a 20-meter circle; likewise for the other end of the circle. It is also difficult for the judge to see

The rider has turned left at E and is crossing the center line at X, where she begins to bend the horse onto a 20-meter circle to the left.

exactly where the circle should come in a large arena, but he can tell basically whether yours is 20 meters in diameter and whether it is egg-shaped or round.

[3]

X Circle right 20 meters
B Turn left

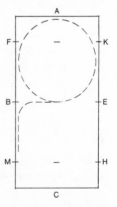

Since this movement requires the same circle you just made but in the opposite direction, these two movements together actually have you ride a figure eight. When you come back to X, in about one horse's length you change the bend to the right and make another 20-meter circle at X. With the previous circle followed by this one, you are riding two precision exercises back-to-back. Don't, however, make your second circle egg-shaped or square just because your first one may have been. You can gain points here by improving the shape of your second circle. Accuracy will be rewarded, but don't just ride the figure. Remember to ride the horse through the circle, keeping him bent to the inside, balanced, and cadenced. Anyone who practices long enough can execute a 20-meter circle; the trick here is to do that plus keep the horse moving as he should be throughout the test.

[4]

C Halt immobile 5 seconds, proceed working walk

This is the first time the tests ask for this downward transition right in front of the judge, and it is also the first time the tests require you to maintain the halt for five seconds. The judge will have an excellent view of your halt from C, so it had better be precise. An inexperienced rider will attempt to halt the horse with his hands, causing the horse to back up or to toss his head. On the other hand, a horse who is in balance and can be driven to a halt will be rewarded here.

The rider should use some half-halts in the turn from M to the short side to get the horse in balance and set him up, then drive him with his seat and back into the halt at C. To ensure your halt is long enough, most judges will silently count to five. The rider should do the same. If your horse starts to move off before the time has elapsed, go with him because he is already moving forward and you have already lost the points. But if your horse is square and standing calmly, it doesn't hurt to keep the halt a few more than five seconds. This shows the judge you have the horse under control and in balance, and can be precise.

After the five-second interval, drive with your seat and back to urge the horse into the walk. Here the judge often sees horses back up, or jig ahead into the walk. You should practice this transition at home, because it's not the easiest one in the book.

[5]

HXF Free walk on long rein
F   Working walk

From C you should ride normally into the corner and then start across the long diagonal from H to F on a free and long rein. If you can show a transition from the working walk to the free walk, it will pay dividends. The sooner you can get the horse to lengthen and lower his stride and frame, the more you will be rewarded. After you reach X, the judge will not be able to see how far the hind foot oversteps the front print, so you should establish the long stride at H if you can. If your horse is still tense from the previous trot-to-halt transition at C or if you have a problem with jigging, the horse is going to show a short walk with no overstep, resulting in a low score for this movement. When you reach

F, you should show another transition back to the working walk. Most riders can do this rather well because they have to pick the horse up to make the turn after F.

[6]

A   Working trot sitting
E–B Half-circle right 20 meters

This movement requires a transition from the walk to the trot at A, which the judge is observing from the side. The horse should flow from one gait to another, without his head coming up. Ride into the corner, then down the long side to E, where you begin a 20-meter half-circle to the right (see diagram).

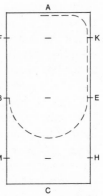

Ride from E to B as though you were on a full circle, coming out 10 meters from X when you cross the center line, and keep the bend.

[7]

B Working canter, right lead, 20-meter circle
B Straight ahead

With your horse already in the proper bend from the previous movement, it should not be too difficult to urge him into a canter and maintain the 20-meter circle, this time making a full circle at B. Remember, however, that the transition occurs precisely at B. The test doesn't allow you a span between two letters to develop the canter, as did earlier tests, so you have to look for the B when you are nearing the end of the arc on your previous half-circle. As you come around to B again, straighten the horse out. He may want to stay bent, because you have ridden the circle one and one-half times. The horse will probably think you want him to stay there unless you tell him otherwise.

[8]

F   Working trot sitting
KXM Change rein

As you approach F on the long side, prepare the horse for this downward transition by making him light with half-halts on the outside rein. Make the transition exactly at F with a nice, balanced sitting trot, and then ride into the corner. Remember that, as we have mentioned before in similar movements, the transition should be made when the horse is straight — parallel to the side of the arena — not when he is bent for the turn in the corner.

Balance the horse on the short side and use your next corner again to lighten him and to prepare him to cross the diagonal. Riding deep into the corner will allow you to set him up on a straight line from K to M. If instead you slide through the corner without an inside bend, the horse will have to make a sudden, sharp bend to come off the wall at K. The beginning of his K–M line won't be straight and he is likely to be unbalanced and on his forehand as he starts across the diagonal. Your score will suffer here, because you are being judged on the accuracy of your line and on how well the horse moves.

When you reach the other side of the arena, make your horse parallel to the side when you come to M, to set him up for the next corner. Ride your horse in a relaxed and balanced manner across the next short side, which takes you only a few meters away from the judge as you pass by. If you are having trouble riding the horse, at least make an effort to bend him into the next corner on the end of the short side. Every time you go by the judge, you want to reinforce the impression that you are a workmanlike rider who respects the need for accuracy in dressage.

[9]

E–B Half-circle left 20 meters

Here we have the same half-circle as in movement #6 of this test, but of course on the other rein. The whole movement this time is nothing but the first half of a 20-meter circle, so it behooves the rider to make it accurate. There are no transitions or supplementary movements here where you can make up any points you lose for a sloppy half-circle. (Some of these dressage tests have portions with too many movements, and others with too few. In this case, it is the latter.) To help your ever-important score for this half-circle, remember to make it round and come 10 meters away from X, using the center line as a guideline.

[10]

B Working canter, left lead, 20-meter circle
B Straight ahead

This portion of the test prescribes the same series of movements off the half-circle as before, this time to the left. Refer to my directives for movement #7 of this test.

[11]

M   Working trot sitting
HXF Change rein

This transition occurs right in front of the judge, facing him. Execute it flowingly, quickly balancing the trot out of the canter. Too often the trot here is strung out and heavy in front, as we frequently see in these lower levels. Get your horse together, between your hand and leg, and ride the corner across the short side to set up the next diagonal from H to F. Again, the horse should move straight across the diagonal, becoming parallel to the side of the arena at F.

[12]

A Down center line
G Halt. Salute.

From F, ride into the corner to prepare for your turn down the center line. Although the horse should straighten out briefly on the short side, you have to ask him to bend to the inside before he reaches A. Otherwise, you will override the center line and will have to make a sharp, sudden turn back onto it, throwing the horse off balance. This will multiply your difficulties at getting a good halt, unless you are adept enough to get the horse back together before you reach G. Your halt in this test comes only six meters in from the judge's position, so here it is even more critical to make it smooth and as square as possible.

I like to see the rider exercise the option to take the halt through the walk, as I have outlined before, because it generally makes for a smoother execution and it shows the judge two transitions — trot to walk, and walk to halt. Since this is the final test in the series at Training Level, it is the last time you will be allowed to take the halt through the walk. Show me you know what you are doing and take advantage of the option, unless you have already developed your horse's trot-to-halt transition sufficiently at home. When you get the halt and the salute, give me a quick smile of showmanship that lets me know you appreciate and respect my efforts in judging the test as much as I do your efforts in riding it.

2. First Level

The First Level tests are progressively more difficult than the previous ones at Training Level. The main difference is the First Level requirement that the horse be "on the bit." Merely accepting the bit, which was adequate for Training Level, will not suffice here.

The reasons are twofold: first, the horse at this point is expected to have gained the balance and schooling required to go on the bit; second, many of the movements introduced at First Level require a degree of collection, which is impossible to achieve unless the horse is on the bit. Therefore, riders who begrudgingly stay at Training Level because their horse "knows how to do First Level movements but won't stay on the bit" are only fooling themselves. The movements undoubtedly are not being done correctly.

In order to understand what the judge expects to see when a horse is truly on the bit, it may help to first know what he or she considers undesirable. If the horse isn't on the bit, he must be either above it or behind it, both of which are unsightly and counter-productive to the aims of dressage schooling.

When a horse is so green that he must be controlled by the rider's physical strength and by the bit in his mouth, he is likely to be above the bit. The application of rein aids causes his head to come up in the air to avoid the harshness of the hands and the bit. The opposite undesirable head position occurs when the horse comes behind the bit, also to evade the pressure. When the rein aids are applied, the horse overflexes at the poll to a point where his forehead is behind the vertical. The horse is then rubber-necked and unable to be controlled.

To cause a horse who is above the bit to lower his head to the proper position — which is with his nostrils about at the level of the rider's knees — the rider must resist the upward movement of the head. Trying to pull the horse's head down will be futile and is likely to aggravate the problem, since the horse was trying to evade your hands in the first place. Instead, any of several techniques may be employed: use slightly more rein pressure; soften the contact by vibrating your fingers on the reins; or use a slight see-saw action that moves the bit back and forth in the horse's mouth. At the same time, you should be driving the horse up onto the bit with your seat, back, and legs to sustain his forward motion.

The opposite techniques must be used if the horse has a tendency to come behind the bit by overflexing and lowering his head too much. In this case the rider needs to use his legs to "push" the horse's head up, by making the horse's hind legs more active. Don't try to pull the head up with your hands, as this would create a false head carriage, causing the bend to be further back from the poll. Such uneducated measures are extremely detrimental to the horse's training.

Of course it is easier to put a horse on the bit if he is already accepting it and going in a Training Level frame. To induce the proper head carriage in a horse who is not fighting the bit, you simply ask the horse to gently flex at the jaw and have a wet mouth. (A horse working with a dry mouth finds the bit in his mouth a brutal instrument.) First, drive the horse up with your legs so that he reaches for the bit. Play with the reins in a gentle give-and-take motion, using a vibrating action so that the horse's jaw begins to relax and soften. As the horse does this, he will usually flex or bend at the poll as he should, bringing his forehead closer to the vertical.

When the horse responds this way and comes onto the bit, reward him instantly by relaxing your elbows and shoulders. Right away take up a lesser feel if the horse continues to carry his head in the proper position, with his nose slightly ahead of the vertical. Be careful not to "throw the horse away," however, by relaxing your contact too much. You should always be able to feel the horse's mouth chewing lightly on the bit through the reins, almost as though you had a minnow softly swimming on the end of a fishing line.

A horse who is on the bit accepts the rider's weight, leg aids, and hands. Therefore he will respond to very slight aids, easily changing his direction or gait without disrupting his equilibrium and balance. Such a horse is totally supple and responsive because of the rapport which has been established between himself and the rider.

This will be next to impossible to achieve unless your seat is supple and independent, allowing you to do what you wish with your hands despite the movements of the rest of your body (and of your horse). A rigid, insecure seat produces hard hands, which will certainly impede the horse's acceptance of the bit. (Can you imagine relaxing your own jaw if someone were jerking a piece of metal in your mouth?) In the long run, the degree of soft or "good" hands will be an almost direct reflection of the rider's basic athletic ability. Therefore, the more time spent at rider-suppling exercises on the longe line, the better chance you'll have of putting the horse on the bit. It will be time well spent, for putting the horse on the bit is like turning the key in the ignition. Until you can do that, you can't properly move the car — or the horse.

If putting the horse on the bit is not that difficult for you, don't congratulate yourself yet. Putting him there isn't good enough; keeping him there is. The judge expects to see the horse remain reliably on the bit throughout the test — not just at the basic gaits of walk, trot and canter, but during all movements and transitions. If you remember to use more leg and seat than hand to ask for each transition (upward or downward), the horse will soon learn to execute them calmly, keeping his head in the proper position. This makes the rider's job considerably easier. When the horse is balanced, supple, and on the bit, your transitions will be smooth, light, and easy to accomplish. You will find, for example, that the horse will go directly from the trot to a square, straight, and balanced halt with minimal use of the aids, all the while maintaining the proper head carriage. For this, the judge will most assuredly reward you.

However, the judge's scrutiny will not be focused solely on the horse's head. He is looking for the whole picture of a First Level horse. In this frame the horse's topline should be slightly rounder and higher than it was at Training Level. The head carriage is elevated and the face closer to the vertical because as the horse progresses in his training, he pushes off with stronger steps from behind (due to a higher degree of engagement) and his forehand is lightened.

In addition to showing the working gaits, the First Level horse must show a lengthened stride at all three gaits, with no change of rhythm. The circles required are smaller — 10 and 15 meters, not 20 meters — so the horse will need to have developed a higher degree of balance. The test movements begin to include lateral work (the leg-yield and the shoulder-in), more advanced bending and precision exercises (the serpentine), and preparatory work for flying changes (the change of lead through the trot).

By writing such movements into First Level, the authors of the AHSA tests have made it very clear that a horse should not leave Training Level until he has done his homework. But these movements should not be overly challenging for the horse, because he should have been schooling in them while competing at Training Level. Since most competitors find it works well to spend one full season showing at any level before moving up to the next one, your horse should have had adequate time to familiarize himself with these movements at home before you ask him to perform them in a more demanding competitive situation.

Perhaps if you have had a successful season at Training Level, you could try riding a First Level test in a small schooling show before doing so at a recognized competition. Dressage schooling shows are scheduled to suit that purpose, often being held in November (shortly after the show season has ended) or in March (just before it begins again). Take advantage of this opportunity to "test the waters" before plunging into First Level. Many judges assume that you (or the horse) have not competed before at the level you are riding in a schooling show, so they may mark you more leniently, scoring your movements one or two points higher than they would in a recognized competition. Although this may serve to encourage the rider, I do not feel it does him or her any good in the long run. You may be in for a shock a few months later when you compete in a recognized dressage competition, if the judge has to tell you your horse is not ready for the level at which he is competing. The time you may have wasted schooling the horse incorrectly could have been better applied toward preparing for First Level, had you been scored against the proper standard to begin with. As in any endeavor, you have to know what you are dealing with before you can expect to succeed at it.

Another difference you should prepare for before riding the First Level tests in competition is the size of the arena. At Training Level, the show committee has the option of designating a small arena (20 x 40 meters) or a large arena (20 x 60 meters) for the tests. From First Level on, the tests must be ridden in a large (Olympic-size) arena. This gives you a longer span across the diagonal and means that you will need to use different markers to visually "spot" the dimensions of your circles. If you do not have a large arena to practice in at home, mark one out in a field. Set up anything that will give you a dry run, so you won't have to cope with the new dimensions for the first time in competition.

AHSA FIRST LEVEL TEST 1

[1]

A Enter working trot sitting
X Halt. Salute. Proceed working trot sitting
C Track right

Since all the First Level tests require you to enter in the working trot sitting, your final warm-up around the test arena should be done mainly in that gait, to get the horse going in a balanced, rhythmic trot. Your seat will need to be more secure to keep your hands from disturbing the horse's mouth; the more you can keep him round and on the bit, the easier you will find it to sit to the trot. One bonus of entering at a sitting trot, however, is that you will be able to use the continuous contact of your seat and legs to keep the horse moving forward and staying straight on the center line.

The halt at X gives our first serious indication of the increased difficulty of the First Level tests. In the previous Training Level tests, you had the option of going from trot to halt with a few walk steps in between. At First Level that is not allowed. The judge expects your horse to be schooled and balanced enough to halt directly from the trot. If he shuffles through it or takes a few walk steps, you will be scored down.

The trot-to-halt sequence can be deceptively difficult to execute, and the only way to enhance your score for this first movement is to practice it well beforehand. If your horse has difficulty when schooling the movement, you can make the transition easier (for yourself as well as the horse) by preparing for it this way: Ride down the center line as though you were starting a test, but don't make a halt at X. Instead, as you approach X, ride a 10-meter circle off the center line to balance the horse. As you are coming off the circle and back onto the center line, then ask for the halt from the trot. Bending the horse this way on a turn makes the trot-to-halt sequence easier.

Practicing with this method encourages the horse to develop the habit of planting one leg solidly at each corner as he comes down from the trot to the halt. Of course you can't use this circle during the test, but you can employ the method in the warm-up area to refresh the horse's memory. If you sharpen his skills this way and he gives you a fluid trot-to-halt transition at the beginning of your test, it is certain to impress the judge and set a favorable tone for the rest of your ride.

The judge will be even more impressed if the halt remains immobile and stationary, with every leg at a corner during your salute. From his head-on vantage point at C, the judge can see clearly whether the horse's front legs are square. It is a bit more difficult for the judge to discern whether the horse's hind legs are square, but he can generally tell if the horse is fairly well balanced from the way he halts. If the horse spreads out behind, the judge can assume that he is not well balanced and therefore is probably not square all the way around.

The key to getting a good, square halt from the trot is to have the horse as light as possible as you come down the center line, using half-halts as you approach X. These will also help keep the tempo of the horse's trot relatively slow and controlled, so that he is not running off through the bridle. If you can make the halt almost completely with your seat, the horse's legs will have a tendency to be driven up from behind and will most likely be square when he halts.

If you fail to accomplish this and you can feel that the horse isn't square underneath you, don't bother trying to correct it. You have already established your score and have lost points for an unbalanced halt, so it is to no avail to try to squeeze one leg or another to square the horse up. Settle for the halt you have, execute the salute, and ask the horse to move off down the center line toward the judge. Just as he did in the previous downward transition, the horse should go directly from the halt to the trot with no walk steps in between as he heads straight ahead toward the judge at C.

Make sure you ride into the corners at C and at M, keeping the horse from popping a shoulder to the inside as he makes the turn. You should always be riding on a rectangle — the true shape of the dressage arena — and not on a steadily diminishing oval, which I see too many riders do.

[2]

B Circle right 15 meters

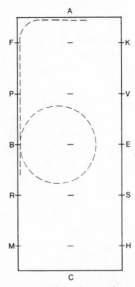

Since the whole arena is 20 meters wide, you should come in five meters from the H–K side of the arena to make this circle (see diagram). Another way to spot your circle in advance is to realize that you must split the 10 meters from X to E, so that you are on the quarter-line. Much of the score for a circle depends on accuracy, so it is an easy way to pick up points if you pay enough attention to where your horse is going. So often judges see horses falling in on the latter half of the circle, which gives you an egg-shaped perimeter rather than a true, round circle. Another common rider mistake here is a circle that does not bisect the B–E line and that does not consist of equal halves on each side: either the rider turns the horse too soon or rides too far past B to initiate the turn. Riding a correct circle is a delicate balance, and you should start your turn with a couple of half-halts to prepare the horse and to balance him into the bend.

This should not be overly demanding, for your horse should have been introduced to turns in the early stages of his training. These turns and circles must initially be large, and as the horse progresses and attains a higher degree of balance they can be steadily diminished in size, from 20 meters down to six meters (a volte). To ride a circle correctly, the horse's spine should comply with the direction of travel and follow the circumference of the circle. The hind feet should follow exactly in the tracks made by the forefeet, and the horse's head should be bent to the inside, so that the rider can see the bulge of the inside eye. In making a 20-meter circle, the horse's inside set of legs has to travel a shorter distance than the outside set of legs. When the circle is reduced to six meters, there is a greater problem of coordination between the inside and outside legs, and it is more difficult for the horse's front and hind feet to follow the same track.

Since the second movement of this test calls for a 15-meter circle, you are putting more demands on the horse than you were in the 20-meter circles at Training Level. So to help the horse with his balance and coordination, your aids become even more important. Use a direct rein on the inside, to keep the horse's head bent onto the circle. Your outside rein keeps him soft and assists with the flexion. Your inside leg provides impulsion at the girth, which helps overcome the tendency of some horses to shorten their stride as they start a turn. Your outside leg, slightly behind the girth, applies pressure to keep the hind legs tracking in the path of the front legs. It also helps prevent the horse's hind leg from describing a larger arc than his inside leg, or from swinging wide with his hind end (tendencies which would be noted unfavorably by the judge).

The judge is looking not only at the shape of your circle, but also at the manner in which your horse executes it. He expects the horse to stay on the bit throughout the circle, engaged and under control, and maintaining the same gait that was intended throughout the turning movement. The circle must be ridden without hesitation, with the horse moving forward willingly and fluidly on the rider's aids, without any loss of cadence as he completes the turn and goes on to the next movement.

[3]

KXM Lengthen stride in trot rising
M   Working trot sitting

Here we have our first requirement in any of the tests for a lengthening, this one done at the rising trot. (If you had any doubt there was a considerable gap between Training and First Level, the three initial movements of this test should have dispelled it by now.) The judge wants to see your horse show as much lengthening as possible, which will depend in part on the horse's innate athletic ability and also on his level of training. If the horse is sufficiently engaged, his hind foot should overstep the front print by at least four or five inches — a generous hoofprint. Some horses at First Level show a six- to eight-inch overstep in the lengthened trot, which can't help but impress the judge.

Along with the overstep, the judge will be observing the overall picture your horse presents in the lengthening. From his side view, the judge should see the diagonal pairs of legs form a parallelogram, with the hind legs reaching under to the same degree that the front legs are extending. If the hind legs do not parallel the front legs, you will lose points because the horse is not sufficiently engaged. When he is engaged, he will show the lengthening the judge wants.

The key to getting a lengthening, then, is in the preparation. The more collection and engagement you can get by using half-halts on the short side as you approach the diagonal, the more lengthening you will

The horse is responding to the rider's aids by lengthening his stride in the trot across the diagonal, which the rider is obtaining here in the rising trot. The horse is in a good First Level frame.

have from K to M. The more precise you can be, showing a lengthening from letter to letter, the higher your score. However, at First Level the judge realizes your horse is probably not well established in his lengthenings and may need part of the diagonal to "invite" him to stretch his frame across it. Therefore, you don't necessarily have to start a full lengthening immediately at K, but you should lengthen out toward X and then gradually come back to a sitting trot at K.

If you know your horse does not have a good lengthening, at least try to create the illusion of one by showing the judge two distinct transitions at K and M. Shorten the trot slightly in the corner before K and then urge the horse to move forward across the diagonal. Again, take him back into your seat and hands a little more than usual as you reach M, so the judge will see a difference in his stride. You may still be marked down for an insufficient lengthening, but at least you have shown the judge you know what is expected of you by showing him two transitions.

You won't gain points, however, by merely rushing across the diagonal and trying to get it over with. The judge can see it coming when a rider goes weakly across the short side, using no preparatory half-halts, and arrives at K with the horse not engaged and moving in an overly relaxed or strung out frame. Invariably at this point the rider suddenly applies his legs while crossing the diagonal, which puts the horse on his forehand and results in a "running trot." The horse is trotting faster, throwing the rider higher out of the saddle, so you may falsely think you are getting a lengthening — until you see your score sheet. In a running trot the stride usually *shortens* and quickens, so the judge will probably give you a 3 or a 4 for such a "lengthening." A poor score will hurt you here, because the lengthened trot has a coefficient of two in this test, which means your score for the movement will be doubled.

A true lengthening has the same rhythm and cadence as a working trot, but the horse covers more ground in the same amount of time because he stretches his body like a rubber band. Since this movement calls for the lengthening to be done in the rising trot, you can only apply the strength of your seat every other beat, driving with your legs each time you sit.

If you have trouble when schooling for the lengthening, refer back to my directives for a practice session at Training Level (p. 5). A particularly helpful method is to ride a 10-meter circle (to lighten, balance, and engage the horse) and ask for a lengthening as you come out of it.

[4]

E Circle left 15 meters

Refer to the guidelines in movement #2 of this test, reversing your aids because here you are on the left rein.

[5]

A Halt 5 seconds, proceed working walk

The halt comes at A, but you should set it up in the corner. Ride into the corner and use half-halts to lighten the horse before driving him into the halt with your seat. Here, as in our entrance into the arena, no walk steps are allowed between the trot and the halt. The judge expects you to hold the halt for five seconds, so he or she will be counting "one-two-three-four-five" silently (as you should be).

From the side view the judge has at C, he can easily discern how well balanced and engaged the horse is in this halt. This is a movement in which you can pick up points if you can make your horse halt square and in balance. Don't fiddle with him, though; if he fidgets or backs up, you will just as quickly lose the points you earned.

After the five seconds the judge wants to see the horse move directly off into the working walk. A nervous horse at this point may have the tendency to jig, be irregular, and maybe do a little pacing or approach pacing. From his side view, the judge can see the horse's cadence and rhythm, so show him your horse's best.

[6]

FXH Lengthen stride in walk
H   Working walk

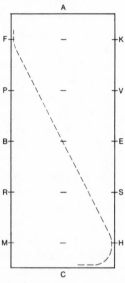

While your horse is being asked to lengthen his stride at the walk, it is just as important to the judge that the horse's gait remain regular and four-beat. He or she will be looking for the horse to swing his neck and shoulders in a relaxed and rhythmic manner, as he engages his hind legs and shows at least a four-inch overstep. Since this is a coefficient movement, the lengthening can pay off in your score. Concentrate on your aids, applying your legs alternatingly, as each shoulder comes back. This is not a free walk, so keep the horse on the bit, but do allow his head and neck to reach slightly down and out as you maintain contact with his mouth.

If your horse is difficult to lengthen in the walk, try at least to create an illusion of it with two distinct transitions (as I discussed earlier in movement #3 of this test). Take care not to override the horse, however. If you urge him too strongly to lengthen and he jigs or breaks into a trot, you're automatically down into the "3" category for a score. Since the requirement here is for the horse to walk, you're better off in the judge's eye if you show an insufficient lengthening rather than a trot.

If you do manage to get a good lengthening from your horse, take advantage of the fact that the lengthening ends at H, which is very close to the judge. Show a marked transition at H, keeping the horse's gait four-beat and regular as he becomes more engaged for the working walk. Some horses here have a tendency to pace a few steps or to approach a lateral movement, which will erase some of the points you earned for a good lengthening. (This is a good example of the intricacy of dressage competition. The key is not in riding the individual movements separately — which many people can do quite well — but riding them in sequence, or putting the test together, which oftentimes seems like a whole different ball game.)

[7]
C Working trot
M Working canter right lead

This movement consists of two progressive upward transitions (walk to trot, and trot to canter), designed to show how light and how flexible the horse is during transitions. You should have ridden the previous corner to set up the first part of this movement, which calls for a transition to the sitting trot right in front of the judge at C. Squeeze gently with your seat and legs a stride or two before C, asking the horse to stay round and in balance and to flow into the trot with his head in the correct position.

Again you should ride into the next corner to set up the second half of this movement, the relatively uncomplicated one-gait transition from trot to canter. Often riders have a tendency to cheat on the corner here, taking a wide turn, because it makes it easier for them to get the horse to take the inside lead. Since the judge can almost reach out and touch you at this point in the test, it is important to execute the movement correctly. Ride deeply into the corner for your turn, so that your horse becomes parallel to the side at M, and then take the canter. This shows the judge how much precision and control you have — two cru-

In the working canter, the rider begins to prepare at R for the next movement, a 15-meter circle at B.

cial factors in riding a dressage test. Don't let your horse become strung out down the long side; maintain the canter but use half-halts to prepare for the next movement (see photo).

[8]

B Circle right 15 meters

This repeats movement #2 of this test, but this time you are in the canter. Refer to my earlier directives on p. 47.

[9]

KXM Change rein
X   Working trot sitting
M   Working canter left lead

As you come out of the 15-meter circle in the previous movement, be sure to ride into your corners to set up the turn across the diagonal. Most horses who are heavy in front at these lower levels plunge into the transition at X, and do a running trot until they are able to balance themselves. As in all downward transitions, the lighter you get the horse in front beforehand, the more you can get him engaged, and therefore, the more cadenced and rhythmical the transition will be.

Concentrate here and make your diagonal accurate. A lot of riders tend to make a sweeping turn at K and almost an S-turn to get to X. Instead, the initial turn you make off the long side should go directly and unwaveringly from K to M, with your line as straight as your entrance down the center line was in the very first movement of the test.

The test calls for the transition to occur right at X. Sometimes if the horse is heavy on his forehand and rushing a bit, he may get ahead of the rider, with the transition to trot delayed until somewhere between X and M. Since this is not precise, it will be scored down.

Usually the upward transition to the canter at M is fairly accurate. Again the horse should be parallel to the long side as you make the transition to the other lead. Ride him into the corners to set up your next movement.

[10]

E Circle left 15 meters

This repeats the fourth movement of this test, so the same directives apply. However, bear in mind that you have already ridden three-quarters of the test by now, so the horse may be a bit tired or losing his concentration. As you prepare for the circle, do a quick spot-check to see whether the horse is still on the aids. If he feels as though he is wilting or becoming disinterested in his work, plan ahead to keep a deep and active inner leg on him in the circle. Otherwise, he may lose some impulsion and be difficult to keep into the canter. Remember, you are not just "riding the test," but also "riding the horse," and you are being judged on both counts.

[11]

FXH Change rein across diagonal
X   Working trot sitting

Be sure again to cross the diagonal on a perfectly straight line, coming to a transition exactly at X. You want the horse to flow into a nice, balanced trot as soon as he reaches X. This is something you have to practice at home, because the long diagonal in a large arena can be rather inviting to the horse, so he may have a tendency to want to sail right across it without making the transition at X. On the other hand, if you practice it too much, the horse may come to anticipate the movement at X. That will surely cause problems later on when the tests call for the horse to canter all the way across the diagonal and take the counter-lead. This exemplifies the principle that the horse must always be listening to the rider, not performing movements from rote memory.

The other problem you may run into here is a flying change of lead at X. If the horse has been schooled for changes at X, he may assume that's what you want when he feels your preparatory half-halts as you approach X. Tell him with your aids that's not what you want, by sitting deep for a downward transition and keeping your legs still. If you inadvertently shift your weight onto the other seat bone at X, a schooled horse may very likely think you are asking for a flying change. (Here we see more of the intricacy of dressage. As you advance to the higher levels, the same aid may mean several different things to the "educated" horse. Therefore, you have to learn how to apply that aid and how to coordinate it with your other aids to convey your exact meaning to the horse.)

[12]

MXK Lengthen stride in trot rising
K   Working trot sitting

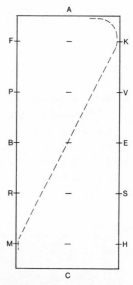

This is another coefficient movement, so give
it your best effort and prepare for it as before,
in movement #3 of this test (p. 48). Since the
test has asked the horse to cross the diagonal
twice without lengthening, he probably won't
be thinking about it unless you are. You have
to do your job here to prepare and guide the
horse through the lengthening, the last demanding movement of this test.

Remember to keep "riding" the horse all the
way across the diagonal, because he may tend
to lose impulsion in the second half of the
lengthening. If the efforts called for in the test
have made him a little less energetic than he was in his previous lengthening, you may find you will need to use your legs more vigorously to
create and maintain the same amount of impulsion.

However, if the horse is not fatigued, you may happily find that he
lengthens better and more easily than before because of the cantering
called for in the previous movement. If you used your time across the
short side to get the horse light, and then apply the added impulsion
already developed through cantering, the horse should lengthen nicely
across the diagonal for you.

When you reach K, sit to the trot and shorten the stride to prepare for
your turn onto the center line, which begins the next — and final —
movement of the test.

[13]

A Down center line
X Halt. Salute.

Here of course we have the "typical" finale to the dressage test. Even
your horse probably knows he is on his way out, so don't let him fall
asleep or conversely try to duck out of the arena prematurely. Ride the
horse actively down the center line, executing a precise trot-to-halt
transition at X (again, no walk steps allowed), and remember that your
job is not over until you finish the salute.

AHSA FIRST LEVEL TEST 2

[1]

A Enter working trot sitting
X Halt. Salute. Proceed working trot sitting
C Track left

Nothing new here. Refer to my directives under AHSA First Level Test 1 for the entrance, but this time you turn to the left at C instead of to the right.

Entering the arena in the working trot sitting, keep your legs evenly on the horse's sides so he will remain straight on the center line.

[2]

E Half-circle left 10 meters, returning to track at H

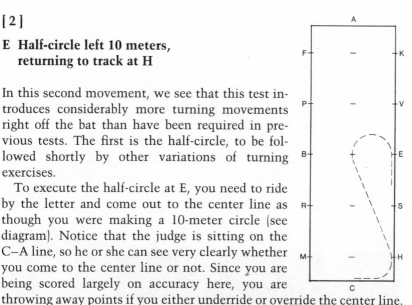

In this second movement, we see that this test introduces considerably more turning movements right off the bat than have been required in previous tests. The first is the half-circle, to be followed shortly by other variations of turning exercises.

To execute the half-circle at E, you need to ride by the letter and come out to the center line as though you were making a 10-meter circle (see diagram). Notice that the judge is sitting on the C–A line, so he or she can see very clearly whether you come to the center line or not. Since you are being scored largely on accuracy here, you are throwing away points if you either underride or override the center line.

Riders often have a tendency to make the half-circle either too small or too large. Spot your path ahead of time, keeping the horse rhythmic and balanced, as you begin to make the circle. Pretend you really are riding a full 10-meter circle until you approach the middle of the arena. Ride to the center line at X and then diagonal back to H. The horse is going straight here (from X to H), or slightly bent to the inside, so you have to change the bend gradually as you make a turn onto the track at H. Your body should be parallel to the long side as you pass the letter H.

When I am judging this movement, I often find that things start to go wrong for the rider at the apex of the half-circle. At this point, a horse will sometimes tend to shorten his stride and slow his rhythm. As the rider struggles to complete the figure, the horse's head may drift to the outside, thereby losing the proper bend and balance — and losing points, as well.

[3]

B Half-circle right 10 meters, returning to track at M

Here we have the same figure as in the previous movement, but on the opposite rein. If you had trouble before, try to pick up points by improving the half-circle this time around. The judge would like to see your riding improve, not degenerate, throughout the test. By riding a better half-circle the second time, you at least show the judge you are aware of your mistakes and know how to correct them. This adds to his impression of you as a thinking, skilled rider, which will be reflected in your score for position and effectiveness of the aids under the collective marks.

The horse is moving well under the rider and is beginning to come off the rail at B to make a half-circle to the right. Notice that both horse and rider are looking in the direction of the bend.

[4]

HXF Lengthen stride in trot rising
F   Working trot sitting

This is a coefficient movement, which merits your extra concentration and effort. You should have used the short side of the arena to get your horse as light and engaged as possible with half-halts, especially in the corners. Then you have a transition both for the horse and the rider — the horse stretches his gait into a lengthened trot, and the rider goes from sitting to rising across the diagonal. The judge wants to see you "get it together" and coordinate your transition with that of the horse, keeping in mind my previously mentioned directives for a lengthening across the diagonal (p. 55).

As you reach F, again you and the horse each have another transition. The horse should be driven back into a working trot as you settle comfortably into the saddle. Then use your corner to balance the horse right away for the next movement, which comes only a few strides away.

[5]

A–C Serpentine of three loops, width of arena

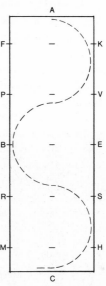

The serpentine is a series of equal curves (20-meter half-circles) from one side of the center line to the other, begun by gradually moving away from the center of one short side and finished by moving back to the track on the opposite short side (see diagram). It is in my estimation a superb schooling and suppling exercise, since it requires a continual change of bend in the horse. The serpentine is also one of the best ways to get an exuberant horse into hand before a test.

Many competitors botch this as a precision exercise in any number of ways: by making their loops unequal in size and shape; by riding a straight line between the ends of each loop; or by riding into the corners as part of the first or last loop. If you study the diagram, you will better understand what is expected of you.

Serpentines cause the horse to change his center of gravity. When he is turning to the left (as he is when he begins the middle loop of this serpentine), the horse must be bent to the left. As he crosses the center line, he becomes perpendicular to it briefly (ideally, for one stride) before he changes his bend to the right to complete that loop and begin the next one.

All this is dependent upon the aids you give the horse, who is relying on you for guidance. Since this movement begins with a turn to the right, the horse should be bent in that direction from the neck all the way back to his tail. You can measure the bend, which you get with a direct rein, by your ability to see the bulge of the horse's inside eye. But to prevent the horse from bending too much, you must keep him on the outside rein. Maintain the impulsion and keep the horse from popping a shoulder to the inside by positioning your inside leg on the girth and driving with it. Your outside leg, slightly behind the girth, keeps the horse tracking his front feet with his hind feet, so he stays on a continuous bend throughout the three loops.

However, "inside" and "outside" are relative terms. Every time you change the direction and the bend in the serpentine, your inside leg becomes the new outside leg, and vice versa. So as you reach the center line, you must use your legs to change the bend so that you can see the bulge of the horse's other eye. The change of bend occurs every time you straighten the horse out for one stride as you cross the center line.

Many riders fail to ride perpendicular to the A–C line for one stride as they cross it, and instead slide by diagonally without organizing their distance. This results in unequal loops. Instead, think ahead that you must split the B–E line in your second loop (see diagram). When a rider starts the middle loop too soon, he has to compensate for it by making his final loop tremendously large. Often such a competitor ends his serpentine by riding into the corner. Since this movement is supposed to end at C, where the judge is sitting, an inaccurate finish will earn you a very poor score indeed.

On the other hand, when it is executed correctly, I feel the serpentine is one of the nicest figures the horse can perform. When it is done flowingly and accurately, most judges find the serpentine very pleasing to the eye, and the competitors find it very pleasing to their score sheet.

[6]

C Halt 5 seconds, proceed working walk

You should have used the curve of the last loop to get the horse light with half-halts in preparation for this halt at C, where you are just about in the judge's lap. You are going from trot to halt at C, which calls for accuracy, balance, and engagement. Hold the halt for five full seconds, or you are not complying with the requirement of the test and you cannot receive the full benefit of a score.

The next part of the movement is a little easier, because it is a one-gait upward transition. It is quite natural for the horse to go from the halt into the walk, so he won't find this as difficult as going from the halt directly into the trot, which was required after your salute at the beginning of this test.

With your horse in the working walk, ride into your next corner to set the horse up for the next movement.

[7]

MXK Lengthen stride in walk
K   Working walk

My directives for riding this movement in the previous test apply. Remember to show a transition to a lengthening as soon as possible after leaving M, using your legs alternatingly. Let the horse's head reach slightly downward but still maintain the contact, with the horse on the bit. Drive him into as long a stride as you can, showing a solid four-beat walk, trying to produce as much overstep as possible.

From a judge's point of view at C, he can evaluate the degree of overstep only until the horse reaches X. After that, the judge's limited vantage point prevents him from observing how long the stride really is. This means if you don't show an overstep right away as you cross the first half of the diagonal, the judge isn't going to see it, so he can't score it well.

Since this is a coefficient movement, it is important to your score that you show a transition back to the working walk at K. This can, to a degree, help atone for a poor lengthening.

[8]

A Working trot sitting
F Working canter, left lead

Your first transition here occurs at A, where you are presented parallel to the judge, so he or she has a full side view of this transition. The judge wants to see the horse flow smoothly into the trot, without his head coming up. The horse should keep his head in the proper frame during the transition and should stay in a rhythmical and cadenced trot. Keep him straight on the short side and then bend him around your inner leg in the corner, so he will be parallel to the long side when you ask for the canter at F. Again, the judge wants that transition to be executed as smoothly as the first one in this movement.

[9]

B Circle left 15 meters

To prepare the horse for this circle, the rider should put him into a balanced canter as soon as possible after he has given the aid at F. Usually when you apply the canter aid to a young, green horse, he tends to jump into the transition and is heavy in front. So when he sees the long side stretch out in front of him from F, the horse may find it inviting and get the idea that he is going to barrel down the long, open expanse. Your aids must tell him otherwise, bringing him together so that he will not scramble out of balance when you initiate the circle. That means using half-halts beforehand and driving with your seat to get him more engaged, so that you can turn onto the circle just as you pass B.

A word about accuracy here: If you start the circle too late, when you are well past B, you may make it too large. If you start it too soon, the converse is true. Start it as you pass the letter and be sure to bisect the B–E line, making equal halves of the circle on each side of that imaginary line. The judge can see clearly whether you correctly split the distance between X and E by having your circle come out to the quarter-line.

If you find you're having trouble balancing the horse sufficiently at the canter for the 15-meter circle, try this schooling exercise at home: ride a few strides at the canter and balance back to the trot briefly. Then move again into the canter and balance back to the trot, working this sequence several times until the horse becomes sharper on the aids. This series of transitions will improve his balance in the canter if you work it into his regular schooling routine.

[10]

HXF **Change rein**
X **Working trot sitting**
F **Working canter, right lead**

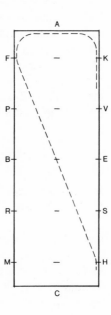

This is the same sequence as in movement #9 of AHSA First Level Test 1, so you may refer to my directives there (p. 53). Keep in mind that after the 15-meter circle at B, you should have ridden the corners on the short side to set up the turn across the diagonal. Ride straight across the diagonal, preparing and balancing the horse with half-halts so that your transition to the sitting trot occurs precisely at X. Keep driving him across the second half of the diagonal so he will have enough impulsion to resume the canter at F. Remember to straighten the horse out and bring him parallel to the long side before making the upward transition to canter.

[11]

E Circle right 15 meters

This circle may be better balanced and lighter than your previous one earlier in this test, because of the amount of cantering the test has called for up to this point. The same considerations apply in this circle as were discussed in movement #9 of this test. This time, however, you are on the other rein.

[12]

C **Working trot sitting**
MXK **Lengthen stride in trot rising**
K **Working trot sitting**

This transition occurs at C, right in front of the judge. As soon as you bring the horse back to a working trot, you have to put him in balance so that you can get some lengthening across the diagonal from M to K. There isn't much time between C and M, so you have to apply half-halts almost immediately, to bring the horse together and make him light in your hands before you turn the corner. If you do this correctly, you will get a lengthening (which is what the judge wants to see) instead of a running trot across the diagonal. As you approach K, show the judge a driving transition back to a working trot. Sit comfortably in the saddle and ride the horse into the corner after K, so he will have a straight approach for your next movement.

[13]

A Down center line
G Halt. Salute.

Use your two turns (in the corner before A and from A onto the center line) to bend the horse properly, so he comes out just to the center line and makes a straight line down it as he heads for G. All the way down the center line, keep your legs on the horse and drive him past X, to keep him from anticipating a halt there as some of the earlier tests required.

Your halt at G comes between M and H, and is six meters in from the judge. He has a good view of whether your horse is square, balanced, and engaged in the halt. Sometimes the center line is mowed in a grass arena, with cross-marks at G, X, and D, which makes it easier for the rider to make sure his body is aligned with the proper letter when the horse halts. I would advise you to practice without markers, in case your test is in a sand arena. But if you find the markers there in a competition, by all means take advantage of them.

AHSA FIRST LEVEL TEST 3

[1]

A Enter working trot sitting
X Halt. Salute. Proceed working trot sitting
C Track right

This is a long test, with 18 movements, so take care not to "ride your horse to death" in the warm-up area, or he may run out of gas before the end of the test. In this test, there are more movements with shorter intervals between each one. Therefore, Test 3 is more demanding on the horse's athletic ability and training, as well as on the rider's concentration. The horse must be sharp, on the aids, and obedient. If he resists during this test, he is likely to make a late transition or even miss a movement completely by the time the next one is called for. So be sure to come into this test prepared, as a driver, not a passenger.

Ride the horse actively down the center line, keeping your legs on him so that he shows some impulsion and engagement. Now that you are riding the latter half of the First Level tests, the judge is going to expect to see your horse move solidly, presenting the correct picture of the way a dressage horse should carry himself.

By now the horse should be on the bit most of the time, and he should have enough balance to make a square halt on the center line at X. From there, you move out at the trot, again showing as much impulsion as possible as you approach the judge at C. Keep the horse moving in a straight line until you make the turn. Since the judge is sitting on the C–A line, he can readily assess your straightness. Horses often have the tendency to "wobble off" into the trot here, usually drifting slightly to the right of the center line and then weaving back onto it before C. This movement calls for the working trot, which is done at a speed of approximately eight-and-one-half to nine miles per hour, so don't move like a slug down the center line.

As you approach C, make a smooth, arcing turn with the horse's head bent to the inside. Be sure to come all the way up to the end of the arena before initiating the turn. Too many riders "cheat" here and turn too soon, which is a quick and easy way to lose points.

[2]

B Turn right
E Turn left

Here the horse makes two turns, each with an angle equivalent to a 10-meter circle. Between the turns, the horse is presented sideways to the judge. This gives the judge the opportunity to assess the horse's gait, so you want to keep the horse moving across the middle of the arena. Horses who trot with a little elegance will, of course, fare considerably better here. If you let the horse piddle along with a short, choppy stride, you have wasted this movement — along with some precious points. Since this is the first solid movement in the test, the rider should use it to make as good an impression upon the judge as possible.

In your first turn, which occurs to the right at B, keep your inner leg active on the girth and ask the horse to bend around it. Slide your outside leg slightly behind the girth, to stabilize the hindquarters and to guide the horse's tracks. Your direct inner rein controls the bend, while your outside rein keeps the horse soft.

In this case, the timing of your turn is crucial. Since you want to end up on the B–E line, you cannot ride by B to initiate the turn (as we did on circles) or you will overshoot the line. The requirement of the test is to ride the B–E line, which calls for precision. You have to begin the turn about five meters before the letter B, so that the equivalent arc of a ten-meter circle from that point would land you right on the B–E line. Many judges make quite a point of this requirement and score infringements severely, so don't overlook it.

As soon as the horse has made the turn from B, straighten him out and head directly across the center of the arena toward E on the opposite long side. While the horse is on that straight line, keep your hands and legs quiet and your weight evenly distributed on your seatbones. On a sensitive horse, the slightest amount of uneven pressure on his sides or back can cause him to drift sideways or even move laterally. Here you aren't asking for that, but rather for the horse to go in a straight line.

To help keep the horse straight, sight the letter E well ahead of time, fixing your eyes on the letter as soon as you make the turn from B. Pretend you want to go head-on into the E, until you are a few strides away. Then begin to prepare the horse for the turn with half-halts. Squeeze gently with your left leg on the girth and your right leg slightly behind it, and guide the horse into a smooth turn back onto the track of the long side.

[3]

A Down center line
L Circle left 10 meters

You have to ride into the corner at K to set up this turn onto the center line. Keep the horse moving and awake, making it clear to him that you are riding down the center line in preparation for another movement — not because the test has ended prematurely. Remember, horses are creatures of habit. Some of them, particularly at the lower levels, think that riding down the center line can mean only one of two things: the test is beginning, or the test is over. It is up to the rider to convince the horse otherwise.

In this instance, make a precise turn (again on the angle of a 10-meter circle) onto the center line, where you will be directly facing the judge. Keep your legs on the horse to keep him moving, but don't let him barrel ahead, anticipating a nonexistent halt at X. Instead you are going to prepare him for a 10-meter circle at L, which is between the letters P and V, 18 meters in from A (see diagram of large dressage arena, above and on p. 207).

Here you have to ride just past L and then continue on a 10-meter circle. This marks the first time the tests have called for a complete 10-meter circle. You and the horse have been preparing for this movement by riding the numerous turns and corners on the angle of a 10-meter circle, and you should obviously have been schooling the 10-meter circle at home for some length of time before expecting the horse to perform it in a competitive situation.

Previously, the tests have called for circles at 20 meters and 15 meters. The difficult part of this circle — or any circle — is to make an accurate, round figure while keeping the horse in rhythm and maintaining the proper bend. A 10-meter circle is more difficult because the younger horses we usually see at this level tend to be heavy in front and can be more difficult to turn. The rider may find the horse less balanced on this smaller circle, so he may falter around the curve.

All the factors we have discussed about previous larger circles (accuracy, balance, suppleness, impulsion, head bent to the inside) apply, but here in the 10-meter circle they become more crucial and more difficult to attain because they require a higher degree of balance in the horse. However, the rider may find a 10-meter circle easier to "spot" than a

15-meter circle, because in this case you know you are riding from the center line out to the long side of the arena for the correct dimensions (see diagram, p. 67). Here you have the edge of the arena to guide you. But remember not to "ride the wall." The circle only comes tangent to the side of the arena for one stride, otherwise you will have a "square circle" — and a low score.

After your circle at L, straighten the horse out again on the center line, and proceed further toward the judge. Get the horse as light as possible in your hands with half-halts to prepare for the next movement.

[4]

I   Circle right 10 meters
C   Track right

This movement mirrors the previous one, except you are making it at the opposite end of the arena and in the opposite direction. The same considerations apply.

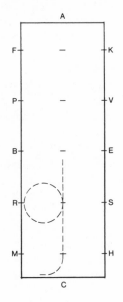

[5]

MXK   Lengthen stride in trot rising
K   Working trot sitting

You should have ridden deep into the turns at C and just before M to set the horse up for this movement, which calls for a lengthened trot across the diagonal. Your half-halts in the corners should have helped engage the horse, which will enable him to lengthen better from M to K.

Unfortunately, judges don't see a true lengthening here as often as they would like to. Instead, the ill-prepared horse may shorten his stride and rush across the diagonal in a running trot. The requirement is to lengthen, which means that the horse expands his body like a rubber band, covering more ground with each stride. By now, the rider should have learned how to apply his legs and seat each time he sits to urge the horse to lengthen, and the horse should clearly know the difference between lengthening and speeding up.

Show as much transition as you can at M, keeping the same rhythm as you cross the diagonal. Again at K, show another transition as you come back to the sitting trot. Unless you can show some semblance of a transition, the judge is going to feel — and justifiably so — that you and the horse do not belong at First Level.

[6]

A   Down center line
L–R   Leg-yield right

Here we go again down the center line. Your horse should have the idea by now that the center line exists for more than the halt-and-salute sequence. At this point the center line is used in the test to introduce leg-yielding, which is the most basic of the lateral movements.

Before we "ride" through the leg-yield as part of this test sequence, it may be helpful to isolate the movement and to gain some perspective on lateral work in general. Unlike more advanced lateral exercises, the leg-yield may be performed without collection. Therefore, it is a suitable exercise for a young or green horse, as it helps teach him to move away from your leg. When the horse has reached a higher degree of balance through training, the leg-yield improves the horse's suppleness and makes him more responsive to the aids.

Overall, the aim of lateral movements such as the leg-yield is to bring the horse's balance and gait into harmony. Lateral work supples all parts of the horse, particularly the quarters and joints, and greatly increases freedom of movement through the shoulder (all of which are extremely desirable and will "pay off" in any work you do afterward).

The leg-yield can be practiced across the diagonal (as in this test) or along the long side or wall of an arena, which is often the best way for a young horse because the barrier helps guide his movement. When performed along a wall, the angle of the horse's body should not exceed 45 degrees from the direction in which he is moving.

One word of caution when practicing the leg-yield or other lateral work: do it only for short periods of time, as prolonged periods may strain the young horse's relatively underdeveloped muscles and may frustrate him mentally as well. Any lateral work should always be followed by some energetic movement straight forward.

In all other two-track lateral movements, the horse is bent uniformly from the poll to the tail; in the leg-yield, he is bent only at the poll. His forehand and hindquarters move on two distinct tracks. While moving on two tracks, the horse's pace must remain regular, supple, and free, maintained by constant impulsion (which, unfortunately, is often lost because the rider is preoccupied with the bend of the horse only). Throughout lateral work, the forehand should always be slightly in advance of the hindquarters (see photo, p. 72).

In this test, the leg-yield is performed precisely from L to R, which means you are moving toward the judge. He will be watching to see that you execute the movement from letter to letter, that the horse is parallel to the long sides of the arena, and that the horse's legs cross over one another at approximately a 45-degree angle as he moves sideways and forward. Keep the horse's body parallel to the long sides of the arena, with his head bent slightly away from the direction of movement, so you can see the bulge of his eye.

The judge wants the horse here to show he is supple and responsive to the rider's left leg. Since we are leg-yielding to the right in this portion of the test, your left leg has to be strong on his side. Oftentimes, if the rider does not use a reinforcing left leg here, the horse will cross over in front but not sufficiently behind. This may cause the horse to drag behind and not stay parallel to the sides of the arena.

To perform a correct leg-yield, the horse must first be in balance. The rider must feel secure that he can put a leg on the horse and have the horse respond to it properly. Many times when the rider applies his legs at this point, the horse resists by coming above the bit and getting strong. The horse mistakenly may get the idea that the rider's legs mean for him to move forward instead of sideways, so he may have a tendency to lurch ahead. So you see, the horse has to be prepared for leg-yielding.

The positioning and use of the rider's aids is critical here. In this movement we are moving toward the right, so you should slide your left leg behind the girth. Your right leg stays on the girth to maintain the forward impulsion. The difficult part is coordinating the pressure and timing of your leg aids, so that the haunches keep up with the front end.

Meanwhile, use your reins to help guide the horse into the movement. Your left rein causes the horse to bend only enough so that you can see the bulge of his left eye. The other rein keeps the horse soft. I sometimes vibrate the right rein to keep the horse from getting too strong and to keep him staying softly in contact with the bit. He should be fully on the bit for this movement, not merely accepting the bit. The lighter you can get him in your hands, the better the leg-yield will be.

Remember that this movement has a coefficient of two, and it is clearly the most difficult task in this particular test. Generally, I find riders do not perform the leg-yield well in competition. So when a judge sees a well-executed leg-yield in this test, he will tend to reward it generously. This movement can allow you to really stand out in the judge's eye, as a thoughtful, skillful, and prepared rider.

[7]

HXF Lengthen stride in trot sitting
F   Working trot sitting

As you finish the previous movement and come around the short side, use that distance from R to H to get the horse light with half-halts. If you can get away with riding a slight shoulder-in (see p. 81) to help bring the horse together, you are likely to get a better lengthening across the diagonal. Remember to show a marked transition at H into a lengthening and at F, come back to a sitting trot. Ask for as much lengthening as your horse is capable of, without overriding him into a running trot or a canter.

The rider is maintaining a good position here as she starts to guide the horse across the diagonal and ask for a lengthened trot. Notice that the horse is covering more ground in one stride than he was in the working trot (see movement #7 of Training Level Test 3).

[8]

A   Down center line
L–S Leg-yield left

Make sure that your turn from A lands you directly on the center line, so you will be properly set up for the leg-yield to the left. If you have to spend your time from A to L wheeling the horse around so that he is straight on the center line, you won't be able to concentrate on getting him light with half-halts. Your leg-yield is bound to suffer from this lack of preparation.

Since this leg-yield is executed to the left, reverse the leg and rein aids as described in movement #6 of this test (p. 70). Go back and read it over, as it takes some time for the full ramifications of two-tracking to "sink in" for most First Level riders. It is not a simple concept, by any means.

If you find your legs are perhaps not strong enough to "convince" the horse to cross over, do not hesitate to use a whip or a spur. Riders often carry a whip in the test but do not think to use it here, when they can so often benefit from the reinforcing aid. When the horse ignores your

General Burton, in a clinic, helps a rider teach a young horse to yield away from the leg. Burton's hand is reinforcing the rider's right leg aid to effect a leg-yield to the left.

leg aid and refuses to cross over, you should meet resistance with resistance and make him move over — be it with your leg, whip, or spur. Once the horse has been persuaded a few times this way to move laterally, it is surprising how fast he will get the idea and decide to cooperate. This willingness to respond laterally is an important attitude to create, for the leg-yield helps prepare the horse for his more advanced lateral work later, some of which comes in the very next test.

[9]

C Halt 5 seconds, proceed working walk

Accuracy is the major factor in this movement, which is performed right in front of the judge at C. He expects the horse to shift down from trot directly to halt, with no walk steps in between. You should time the halt so that it occurs when your body is precisely at C.

While precision is important, it is not enough. The horse must also be balanced and engaged as he comes to a square halt. If he is square in front but not behind, settle for that and concentrate on keeping the horse stationary and immobile for five full seconds. Trying to square a horse up after he has halted usually creates worse problems, such as moving sideways, backing, or fidgeting.

After the five seconds, move the horse forward into a working walk. Make an effort to make this a solid transition, driving the horse onto the bit and into a four-beat walk with a marching tempo. If you just shuffle ahead into a listless walk, the picture you present to the judge is somewhat less than impressive.

[10]

MXK Lengthen stride in walk
K   Working walk

As in our previous discussions on lengthening, you want to get as much out of the horse here as possible. Use your seat and legs alternatingly, squeezing with your left leg as the horse's left shoulder comes back, and with your right leg as the horse's right shoulder comes back. This helps the horse move from behind, so he should show a better overstep, which is what the judge is really looking for here. A six-to-eight-inch overstep would be considered quite good.

A tense horse might tend to jig here, which will cause him to be irregular in his steps. The judge will mark this down as insufficient (4) or below. As a competitor, you cannot afford too many insufficient scores for the individual movements, or your final percentage will be below 50 percent. At that rate, the judge will feel you should go back and do some homework before competing again at this level.

[11]

A Working trot sitting
F Working canter left lead

This movement calls for two successive upward transitions, which at this point should feel like a bit of a breather to you (and to the horse). At A you drive the horse smoothly from the working walk into the working trot, taking care to keep him on the bit, relaxed and in the proper frame. Immediately you must begin to organize your space, riding the horse into the corner and preparing him for the canter, which comes at F. After the corner, straighten the horse out so that he is parallel to the long side, and time your aids so that he takes the canter when your body is at the letter F. The horse should flow into this transition smoothly, moving straight ahead down the long side.

[12]

B Circle left 10 meters

You see the transitions in this test come in rapid succession. From F, where the horse has just taken the canter, he has only a few strides down the long side before he has to initiate the turn for a 10-meter circle at B. This is the first time the tests have called for the horse to make a circle of this size at the canter, which requires considerably more balance and suppleness than did the 15-meter canter circles in the previous test.

To perform this circle accurately, the rider must pass B to start his turn, then stay on a circle and come around to X, continuing on the circle back to B. When you reach B, the horse should be parallel to the long side once again. If you will do this, you have a better chance of the circle being round. Judges sometimes count the number of strides on each half of your circle, and more often than not they find a stride "missing" on the second half, which gives you an egg-shaped circle.

It's fairly difficult to "spot" the outer dimensions of this circle (toward A and C), so the rider should have a good feel for the size of a 10-meter circle before he tries to ride the figure in competition. From B, the next letter down is R, which is 12 meters away. The circle comes out five meters in that direction, which can only be described as "less than half the distance between B and R" — a rather imprecise definition, to be sure. If it is difficult to describe, it is even more taxing to ride accurately. No one ever said this sport was easy.

[13]

H–K Lengthen stride in canter
K   Working canter

This is a coefficient movement, which calls for you to lengthen the horse's canter on the long side and then bring him back to a working canter. So often, judges see one of two things here: either nothing happens, or the rider almost gets run away with. You have to strike a happy medium between those two extremes, asking the horse to expand his body like a rubber band instead of merely speeding up. As in the lengthened trots previously asked for in this test, the horse's tempo should not change. He should just cover more ground with each stride.

I would prefer to see a rider overdo the movement than to do nothing by just continuing in a weak canter. I want to see the horse really move out and stretch through the body, which can be a dramatic, breathtaking sight that will earn you points.

To get this response from the horse, you must sit deep, using your legs and thighs (and spurs if necessary), all the while driving the horse forward with your seat into the bit. If you have trouble getting a lengthening at the canter, try this schooling movement at home: Ride a 20-meter circle at the working canter. Remaining on the circle, ask the horse to do four or five strides of lengthening, then bring him back to the working canter. The circle gives you a better opportunity to put the horse in balance and to gain more control. When the horse becomes more responsive to your aids on the circle, go down the long side and work on his canter lengthenings there.

[14]

FXH Change rein, at X change of lead through trot

Since you have just lengthened the horse in the previous movement, he's bound to be slightly heavy on his forehand at this point. Use the corners and the short side to balance and lighten him with half-halts, so that he will be more engaged as you make the turn at F. Continue to use half-halts as you ride across the first half of the diagonal, so the horse will still be light when you ask for the transition at X.

Be sure to make the transition to the trot with your seat rather than your hands, otherwise the horse is likely to come above the bit and not stay straight. He should relax into two or three strides at the trot, while remaining on the bit and straight on the diagonal, and then flow back into the canter on the other lead.

The rider's aids are crucial here. As you head across the first part of the diagonal on the left lead, the horse is ever so slightly bent in that direction (although he must be moving in a straight line). Your left leg is active on the girth, and your right leg is slightly behind it to stabilize the hindquarters. At X, during the few trot steps, you straighten the horse (and your aids) out, so that when you reverse your leg aids to ask him for the right lead, he changes his bend accordingly.

Since a lot of young horses are heavy when they drop from canter to trot, they may tend to go into a strong trot at X, which will really get you in trouble in this movement. To work on overcoming this tendency at home, I ride the horse on a 20-meter circle, working canter-trot-canter transitions (two or three strides at each gait) several times over. This way, the horse learns not to get frightened or excited when he drops from canter to trot, and it teaches him not to go into a running trot during the transition. After I've worked the horse this way on the circle and he seems fairly content with it, I'll come across the diagonal to see whether my schooling will carry over on the straightaway (as the test requires). If it doesn't, a few more sessions on the circle — interspersed, of course, with some work on straight lines — should improve matters.

Some horses, instead of being hard-headed about the change of lead through the trot, quickly learn to anticipate it, which must be avoided. Especially if you have been schooling the horse in flying changes at X, he may even decide to skip the trot interval between leads entirely during this test. Although the flying change is a more advanced version of the movement, it has to be scored as insufficient here because the test requires some trot steps at X. The horse has to be obedient enough to listen to the rider and to comply with the aids, without being a "show-off" (as some competition horses are) and doing more than is being asked for. If you know your horse has this tendency, you will have to be particularly clear and strong with your aids as you approach X, taking care to sit still in the saddle. If you shift your weight or legs, the schooled horse may, with good reason, interpret that as the aids for a flying change. This is a good example of why a rider must try to put himself into the horse's frame of mind — to "think like a horse," if you will.

[15]

B Circle right 10 meters

[16]

K–H Lengthen stride in canter
H   Working canter

[17]

MXK Change rein, at X change of lead through trot

I have lumped these three movements together because they parallel the same sequence we just performed in movements #12, #13, and #14. This time, of course, we are on the other rein. The only other directive that bears mentioning here is that since you are now near the end of a very long test, the horse may be tiring. Between movements, take a quick spot-check with your aids to assess whether the horse is still listening, concentrating, and moving forward. If he is not, a little cue to wake him up (maybe a spur or a few half-halts, if you can do it subtly) will help him make it through this last demanding series of movements.

[18]

Between K & A Working trot sitting
A   Down center line
X   Halt. Salute.

If the horse has become heavy during the previous movement, the rider may have difficulty getting him back to the trot in the first part of this movement. Luckily, the test is generous enough to allow you the distance of an entire corner to get the downward transition, instead of requiring it to be performed precisely at the letter. If you expect you may have trouble with your horse here, start asking for the trot right away at K. Otherwise, he may still be cantering when you approach the center line, and you will have to abruptly bring him down to a trot. This would disrupt the flow of the entire movement. Instead, the judge wants to see a smooth, flowing transition at X, where you halt and salute.

AHSA FIRST LEVEL TEST 4

From this test onward, all trot work is done sitting unless specified otherwise. At this stage of the game, the horse is expected to have enough balance to cope with the rider's constant weight on his back. The horse should also be learning to move in collection, which requires the contact and influence of the rider's seat.

First Level Test 4 is used as the qualifying test for the AHSA annual awards for Champion First Level Horse. In this case, you may have the test read to you during a regular competition. However, if the horse does qualify here and goes on to compete at the USDF regional finals in the fall, the same test must be ridden from memory.

Clearly, this is not a simple test, since it is used to determine the top horses regionally and nationally at First Level. It is, as it was designed to be, the most difficult test at this level. Its movements bridge the gap between First and Second Levels. In fact, portions of this test are very similar to the former (1979) AHSA Second Level Test 1. In an effort to upgrade the standards of dressage in this country, the test committee has seen fit to introduce some of the more difficult movements (particularly lateral movements and smaller circles) towards the end of the First Level tests.

[1]

A Enter working trot
X Halt. Salute. Proceed working trot
C Track left

All my previous directives on the entrance and salute on the center line apply here. By now, both you and the horse should have ridden enough tests to enable you to make a straight and accurate entry onto the center line at A, with a square and balanced halt at X. Your salute should be polished, balanced and showmanlike. You should then organize your reins immediately and move the horse directly into a flowing trot, riding him all the way to the end of the arena and turning smoothly to the left onto the track in front of the judge at C. Since you are not at the beginner stage anymore, the judge will expect more out of your overall performance. Establish the fact right away in this first movement that you are a thinking, skilled, and workmanlike rider who knows his job — and knows how to get the optimum performance from his mount.

If your horse resists (first photo) as you enter in the working trot, use the distance along the center line to correct him, as this rider has, and to bring him into the proper First Level frame (second photo).

[2]

E Circle left 10 meters

As in the previous test at this level, all the circles here are 10 meters in diameter. The circle should be round, rhythmical, and balanced. Be sure to come out just to the center line, which should not be hard to do if you are riding in a grass arena where the center line has been mowed. In a sand arena, the horses who rode this test before you may have in effect "marked out" the dimensions of the 10-meter circle for you with their hoofprints. Don't follow their marks unless they lead to an accurate circle, however. Otherwise, it is like following a drunken driver through the fog — you may end up going over a cliff right behind him. On the road and in the dressage arena, it is wiser to make your own way unless you are absolutely confident that the path ahead of you is the correct one.

[3]

E–K Shoulder-in left

As you come out of the circle in the previous movement, you are already on the correct bend to begin this one. It is important to pay extra attention to the latter part of your 10-meter circle, because if it is inaccurate or if the horse is not together, you will not be able to perform the shoulder-in correctly. The movement in itself is difficult enough, so don't complicate matters by starting it off wrong. You need to flow directly into this movement as soon as you finish the circle at E (see diagram).

Before I discuss the shoulder-in from a judge's viewpoint, let me address the movement generally so the rider knows what he is dealing with. Along with many other trainers, I consider the shoulder-in the foundation of the other lateral movements. It is also one of the more effective ways to supple a horse — particularly an exuberant one — who needs to be softened and brought back into hand before a competition or before a more advanced training session.

The term "shoulder-in" means what it says: the horse's shoulder faces the inside of the arena. His inside front leg passes and crosses in front of the outside leg. The inside hind leg is placed in front of (but does not cross) the outside hind leg. The horse's body is bent away from the direction of travel, but at not more than a 30-degree angle.

This is a three-track movement. The horse makes the tracks with: 1) his inside front leg; 2) his outside front leg and inside hind leg; and 3) his outside hind leg.

The most common schooling method of initiating a shoulder-in begins on the corner, as you turn from the short side of the arena. As the horse continues the bend onto the long side, the rider lets him take exactly one step off the track with his front end. Instead of straightening the horse as you normally would along the long side, you maintain the bend as the horse moves with his forehand off the track but keeps his hindquarters on it.

The rider must drive the horse forward on this bend, keeping the horse's head to the inside so you can see his inside eye. Your outside rein, working as an indirect rein towards the inside haunch, prevents the horse's neck and shoulders from overbending. Your inside leg, strong on the girth, drives the horse continually forward onto that outside rein while your seat helps maintain the impulsion. Your outside leg, behind the girth, controls the degree of bend in the horse's body. The skillful coordination of these aids will cause the horse to supple as he bends his entire body around your inside leg, moving smoothly on three tracks down the straightaway.

If instead the rider pulls the whole head and neck too far to the inside — a common error — the horse will be out of balance and will not be on three tracks. (Remember that you are driving the horse from the rear to the front into the movement, not pulling him into it from the front to the rear.) If the horse bends in the neck but not through the body, none of his legs will cross as he moves down the long side; if there is no bend in the neck or the body, both his hind legs and front legs will cross. Both results are incorrect.

In the shoulder-in, the body should be bent uniformly from the poll to the tail, with only the front legs crossing as the horse moves laterally. The hind legs continue to move forward, but do not cross over.

When executed in this fashion, this movement functions as a collecting device. Each time the horse takes a step in the shoulder-in, he moves his inside hind leg underneath his body and places it in front of his outside leg. In order to do this, he must lower his inside hip, which induces collection.

In this specific test movement, the shoulder-in is performed off the circle, from E to K. As you approach K, straighten the horse out so that he is parallel to the long side. Bend him into the corner, straighten him out for the short side, and again bend him into the next corner to set him up for the next movement.

[4]

FXH Lengthen stride in trot rising
H   Working trot rising

Show an obvious transition at F and ask the horse for as much lengthening as you can get without risking him breaking into a canter. Since this is executed here at the rising trot, you can only apply the pressure of your aids as you sit for every other beat. Take care to even out the pressure as much as possible, or you may cause the horse to be uneven in his lengthening. At H, show another transition back to the working trot (sitting).

[5]

B Circle right 10 meters

This parallels the second movement of this test, but this circle is done on the right rein.

[6]

B–F Shoulder-in right

Re-read my directives for movement #3 of this test. It will probably take some time for your horse (and perhaps for his rider as well) to get the "knack" of performing a proper shoulder-in. This can be rather strenuous on the horse's muscles, so in schooling do not work on the shoulder-in for extended periods of time. Always follow it up with some energetic work on straight lines.

Another use of the shoulder-in schooling comes into play when the

The correct angle in the shoulder-in. Notice that the horse is moving on three distinct tracks.

horse tries to run off with you when you ask for a downward transition from canter to trot. If you immediately put him into a shoulder-in, he will have to balance himself rather quickly in the trot.

[7]

A Halt 5 seconds; proceed working walk

The rider's body should be at the letter A when you make the halt. The horse should go directly from trot to halt, square and in balance. If the horse shows a few walk steps in the transition, the judge will deduct at least one point from your score. If the walk is prolonged, you will lose even more points.

With the horse immobile, count slowly (and silently!) to five. Then ease the horse into a working walk and ride into the corner.

[8]

K–H Lengthen stride in walk
H   Working walk

Now we come to a new movement in the tests: a lengthening on the long side. This is a very difficult movement for a judge to evaluate, because the horse is moving on a straight line toward him. To score the movement, the judge needs to see how much overstep the horse has in his walk. In this case, it is almost impossible for the judge to view the overstep until the very last part of the movement, because of his position at C. Were the horse being presented sideways to the judge, it would be a different story — and in my opinion, a better test.

[9]

C Working trot
M Working canter, right lead

At C, where he can just about reach out and touch you, the judge wants to see the horse make a smooth, flowing transition from the working walk to the working trot. He will mark you down severely if the horse resists by tossing his head up and lurching forward into the trot.

You have only a short distance (half of the short side and one corner) to prepare for the working canter at M. Be sure to straighten the horse out first along the long side before giving him the canter aid; otherwise, you show the judge a lack of precision. The horse should flow into the canter transition as smoothly as he was expected to into the trot in the first part of this movement. Many horses, when they take the canter here, have a tendency to fall in towards the center of the arena and then shift back onto the track. Keep your inside leg on the horse, to keep him bent properly.

[10]

B Circle right 10 meters

This is our third 10-meter circle in this test (to be followed by yet another), taken from the midpoint of the long side. Now that you are riding the latter half of the test, your horse may be tiring somewhat and may require more vigorous pressure from your inside leg to maintain his impulsion through the circle. Make sure your circle really ends back at B, and that you are not still turning when you come around to the letter again.

[11]

K–H Lengthen stride in canter
H   Working canter

This is a coefficient movement. Again, as in movement #8 of this test, it is difficult for the judge to assess the lengthening from his limited, head-on vantage point at C. However, do show as much lengthening as you can right away when you begin the movement at K. Emphasize the transition back to a working canter at H, where you are close to the judge, by making the horse come under and back in balance. The sooner you balance him here, the better off you will be for the next movement.

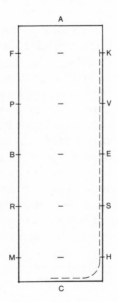

[12]

MXK Change rein, at X change of lead through trot

You are only asked to perform this movement once in this test, instead of twice as in the previous test at this level. Get the horse as light as possible with half-halts as you begin to cross the diagonal. At X, in the center of the arena, use your seat to make the brief transition down to the trot. Keep the horse on the bit and in the same frame for the two or three steps at the trot, then urge him gently back into the canter on the other lead. Pay attention to the horse's path across the diagonal, for straightness is important to the judge here. Ride the horse so that you and he are parallel to the side of the arena at K, which will set up the next corner for you.

[13]

B Circle left 10 meters

[14]

H–K Lengthen stride in canter
K   Working canter

I lump these two movements together for two reasons: first, to avoid being repetitive about the 10-meter circle; and second, because the circle sets you up very nicely for the lengthening on the long side. If you make your circle round, cadenced, and rhythmical, flowing out of the bend into straightness on the rest of the long side, your horse should be moving in a good working canter. Keeping that gait, ride into the corner and shorten your horse somewhat as you pass C, to collect him for the next corner. Then, drawing on the impulsion he established earlier coming out of the circle, he should be eager to lengthen his stride at your command on the next long side, from H to K. Here he is moving away from the judge, who has a much better opportunity to observe his gait than in the previous canter lengthening in the opposite direction.

This lengthening is another coefficient movement, so you really want to urge the horse to stretch his gait through the body. Make it dramatic and energetic. If you can throw a little dirt on the judge's score card at this point, that's a good sign that the horse is really digging in and lengthening his stride.

At K, make a solid transition back to the working canter. You need to get the horse back into balance right away here, because the next transition comes very rapidly.

[15]

A   Working trot
FXH Lengthen stride in trot
H   Working trot

At A, bring the horse smoothly into a downward transition from the working canter to the working trot (sitting). He needs to be light in front and balanced. If instead he is heavy on the forehand, his "lengthening" across the diagonal is likely to be a running trot. At H, bring the horse back into a working trot. Ride him into the corners and then straighten him on the next long side.

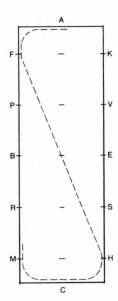

[16]

B Turn right
X Turn right
G Halt. Salute.

This is a most unusual sequence for the final movements in a test at this level. It is the first time you finish a test without riding directly down the whole center line. The horse may be somewhat fatigued at this point, and perhaps slightly annoyed that he is not yet riding down the full center line to finish the test. So the rider has to be especially awake here, to guide and support the horse.

As you come up the long side and approach B, turn to the right slightly before you reach the letter so that the horse comes straight onto the B–E line. Repeat this maneuver just before X, so that the horse ends up straight on the C–A line. You will need to keep your legs on the horse to get enough impulsion to finish the short ride down the center line to G, where you come directly from the trot to halt and make your salute.

3. Second Level

There comes a very obvious demarcation between the tests at First and Second Level. From this point on, the horse is expected to look and move like a confirmed dressage horse, with a round back, an elevated topline, and a rhythmic gait.

The requirements of the Second Level tests are more difficult, calling for work at the collected and medium gaits (instead of working gaits and lengthenings). The horse is asked to perform a precise rein-back and more advanced movements including the half-turn on the haunches, the travers (haunches-in), and the counter-canter.

These movements are impossible to perform unless the rider has had the patience and diligence to develop an effective seat. Until you have a flexible seat that is "in" the horse — not "on" the horse — and until your seat is so secure that your hands are not influenced by what's going on with your body, you are a beginner and are not capable of training a horse. The idea of a green rider on a green horse is preposterous and always has been.

Therefore, a person competing at Second Level must be a rider, not a passenger. Too much of our time in this country is spent trying to advance in the levels without developing the first fundamental — the rider's seat. In Europe, riders spend their first six months without stirrups, usually on a longe line and mostly at the sitting trot. That way, the rider becomes supple and deeply seated in the saddle, giving him the great strength of seat that will sustain him when he asks for extensions or lateral movements. Only this type of rider will be able to perform the demanding movements which follow in the Second Level tests.

AHSA SECOND LEVEL TEST 1

[1]

A Enter working trot
X Halt. Salute. Proceed working trot
C Track right

As in previous tests, the judge expects your horse to enter on a straight line and to halt square and balanced. Your entrance should be straight, with the horse in balance. The rider should have prepared the horse so that he is responsive to the legs and seat and moves freely forward. He should be in balance, in the proper frame, and on the bit.

The transition at X is trot-to-halt. The horse should stay straight and remain in balance with each leg on a corner. He must remain immobile as the rider makes the salute. Then you proceed from halt to trot and move absolutely straight ahead toward the judge at C, where you turn the corner as though you were riding a 10-meter circle.

[2]

B Circle right 10 meters

My previous directives apply here: make the circle round, come all the way out to X, and be sure when you turn off the center line that the horse doesn't pop a shoulder to the inside. He should be bent and follow his bend as he makes the circle. Also, a horse may have a tendency to shorten his stride as you make him turn. Try to keep your inside leg on him so he maintains his stride and keeps a nice round 10-meter circle.

[3]

B–F Travers right

As you come to the last strides of your circle, you prepare for a travers, which was not in the old tests at this level. The travers is actually a haunches-in, which is in effect a half-pass on a straight line.

When executing the movement, the hind end of the horse comes off the track about one horse's width, and he moves on three tracks. The horse is bent from the ears to the tail, just as in a half-pass. The problem is to have the horse bent not only in the neck and shoulders, but in the body as well. He should be crossing over with his front *and* hind legs as he moves laterally, maintaining the same angle all the way from B to F.

Since the horse is expected to remain on the bit, you should be able to see the bulge of his inside (right) eye. Keep the same rhythm and cadence as in the trot that you had developed in the circle in the previous movement.

Just before F, straighten the horse out to make the turn, being sure to show as distinct a transition going out of the travers as you did going into it.

The most common problem in the travers, from the judge's viewpoint, is seeing the horse's head and neck bent but not the body. You also sometimes see the opposite problem, with the horse overbent and making four tracks. I find that less of an error than having the horse not bent through the body. In some cases the back stays straight and the horse resists and backs off, refusing to stay in the rhythm or on the bit.

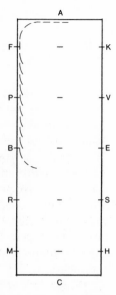

This is a difficult lateral movement, made even more so by its placement so early in the test. Since it carries a coefficient of two, a poor mark here will hurt your overall score considerably.

The travers right, as seen from the rear. Here the swishing of the horse's tail indicates resistance, which will lower the score for this movement.

[4]

KXM Medium trot rising
M   Working trot

Since you have used the travers to collect your horse a bit, you should reinforce that with half-halts across the short side to get the horse as light as possible in your hands as you approach the corner before K. Then sit deep and drive as you cross the diagonal, asking for as much medium trot as you can each time you sit.

It may be difficult for you to feel when you have a good medium trot unless you have practiced riding the gait under the eye of a knowledge-able person on the ground. Your trainer will be able to evaluate your medium trot the same way a judge will, by looking for the amount of engagement from behind as evidenced in the horse's length of stride.

Some horses are able to overstep each front print by as much as six to ten inches, which will impress the judge if the horse is achieving it by stretching through his whole body. If he is not sufficiently engaged behind, the horse may only replace his front print with his hind one, or he may fling his front legs out into what judges call a "flip-flop" trot. This occurs when the horse points his front toe way out in the air when lengthening but his foot lands behind the point where the toe was pointed. The high action in front may make a dramatic impression on

Here in the working trot, the rider guides the horse deep into the corner after M. Notice that she is looking ahead and that the horse is in a Second Level frame.

the spectators, but the judge would rather see the horse engaged and reaching with the same angle from behind as in front.

When you reach the letter M, be sure to show a transition back to working trot sitting. This transition should be even more obvious than the one in previous tests from a lengthened trot to a working trot, because the horse should have been moving forward more and covering more ground in each stride of his medium trot. You are close to the judge when you make this downward transition at M, so a rider who can drive her horse down to a balanced working trot sitting will certainly improve her score here (see photo).

[5]

E Circle left 10 meters

The judge wants your circle to be round, cadenced, and balanced, as in our previous circles. This time, as you come off the circle at E, don't straighten the horse out as you normally would when you reach the long side. The bend you have established in the 10-meter circle has set up the horse properly to ride right into the next movement.

[6]

E–K Travers left

To initiate this movement, slide your outside (right) leg behind the girth, keeping the horse bent to the left just as he was on the circle, and causing him to move onto three tracks for the travers (haunches-in). At the same time you are guiding the horse into position, don't forget to pay attention to the manner in which he is moving. He should maintain the same rhythm, cadence, and balance as he had on the circle.

I find that most horses enjoy the travers, and they learn to do it fairly quickly if the rider's seat is strong enough. The driving aid in this case is the rider's inside (left) leg on the girth, which causes the horse to move over. The supporting aid, which causes the horse to bend, is the outside leg behind the girth. This aid will need to be strong only if the horse resists the bending. If the horse is light, supple, and cooperative, you won't need to use much outside leg. But in any case, the rider's inside leg must remain active to keep the horse moving forward.

At K comes a transition out of the travers, so you must make the horse straight, parallel with the long side of the arena. Then bend him into the corner and straighten him out again on the short side to prepare for the next movement.

[7]

A Halt, rein back 3–4 steps, proceed at working walk

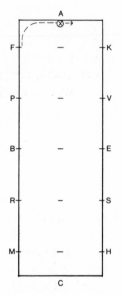

This is the first time the tests have called for backing, which may sound easy but isn't. Too often in this test, judges see the horse resist in any number of ways, all of which are undesirable and are grounds for deducting points: the horse becomes heavy on the forehand and his head goes up above the bit while he backs crooked, or doesn't back by diagonals, or shuffles backwards in a shortened stride and drags the hind feet. It doesn't make for a very pretty picture.

You have to practice backing. Horses aren't any more accustomed to walking backwards than we are, so you cannot expect them to do it smoothly and gracefully by nature.

The rein-back is the type of movement that can get you in trouble, which is one reason I believe it is introduced at Second Level, when a rider should be able to cope with backing movements. After horses learn the rein-back, many of them get the idea that they should back up every time they halt. So you have to be sure of your discipline once the horse learns to back.

For me, the most effective way to train a horse to back has been to have someone on the ground with a whip. You halt with the horse in balance and then ask him to back up. If he resists, the ground person applies light pressure with the whip on the horse's lower front legs until he obeys. You may have to work this over and over again: Halt, ask the horse to back three or four steps (as this test requires), and then move the horse forward into the walk.

As you can see, you have to know what you are doing to teach the horse to back quietly and obediently. Just sitting there and pulling on the reins won't do it. You have to use your seat at the same time as you apply the rein aids alternatingly (left rein, right rein, left rein) to get the horse to stay on the bit as he backs by diagonals. Your legs have to stay on the horse's sides to keep him balanced and obedient.

Notice that the test calls for you to back three or four steps and then move immediately forward into the walk. Don't make the mistake of halting after your final backwards step. If the horse squares up from the diagonal, that counts as another step.

[8]

FXH Medium walk
H   Working walk

The medium walk shows more length of stride than a working walk or a lengthened walk, but less than an extended walk (which comes at Third Level). More important than trying to achieve a specific number of inches in the overstride is to show a difference between your horse's working and medium walk. In practicality, you just ask for as much lengthening of stride as you can get in the walk, without pushing so hard that the horse breaks into a trot.

The judge will be looking to see that the horse maintains the four-beat walk rhythm and doesn't jig (if he does, your score will be insufficient or lower, for irregularity). He wants to see the horse relaxed, marching forward, and overstepping with his hind legs. The horse should reach down and forward onto the bit, showing no disruption in his head carriage during the transition into or out of the medium walk.

Be sure to walk a straight-as-an-arrow diagonal from F to H, where you collect the horse back into a working frame.

[9]

C Working canter, right lead

The earlier tests have asked you to take the canter from the trot; now the requirement is to move directly from the walk into the canter. The transition is more difficult this way, because the horse needs to have achieved a certain degree of collection and balance in order to do it correctly.

The horse should remain relaxed, without his head coming up, as he takes the canter depart right at the letter C. Since you are just about in the judge's lap here, any resistance or trot steps will be glaringly evident to him (and to you, when you read your test sheet).

[10]

B   Circle right 10 meters

All the directives I've given for previous circles apply here. Remember to use your inside leg at the girth to maintain the impulsion. Your outside leg, slightly behind the girth, helps the horse's hind leg to follow his front tracks. If you don't keep your outside leg behind, the horse may have a tendency to throw his hind end to the outside of the circle. If you have the opportunity to practice this movement on freshly dragged dirt footing, go back afterwards and look at your horse's hoofprints to see if the hind prints make a wider circle than the front ones.

[11]

K–H   Lengthen stride in canter
H   Working canter

Lengthenings are a way to gain points easily, so a rider should take advantage of this. The way to improve your score is to make obvious transitions in this movement, first at K, as the horse lengthens out, and again at H, where he shortens and comes back into the working canter.

Many riders, some of whom may be too timid to let the horse really move forward into a lengthened canter, have a tendency to just sit there and wait for it to be over. They are losing points every step of the way for an insufficient lengthening, and there is really no excuse for it.

Instead you should drive the horse into a lengthening, causing him to come under himself and stretch his entire frame with each stride, in an energetic but obedient manner. He must not plunge into the lengthening on his front end with his mouth open, nor should he resist coming back into a working canter. Gentle half-halts and an adjusted seat as you approach H should bring him back; if not, use stronger aids to make the horse listen to you.

[12]

MXK   Change rein; change of lead through trot at X

After you ride the short side you immediately cross the diagonal again. If your horse tends to anticipate, he may try to move into another canter lengthening as soon as you straighten him out and head across the diagonal. Be alert and use half-halts to prepare the horse for the idea that something else is in store for him this time.

After he listens to your half-halts and you feel him lighten, drive with your back and seat to get a soft, flowing transition down into the trot. After the horse takes two or three trot steps, apply the aids for a left-lead canter. While you are doing this, keep in mind that the entire series of transitions should be made on a straight line. Often judges see a weaving S-turn here as the horse brings his head up and makes an unbalanced transition into a running trot and then into a canter that is heavy on the forehand. A little attention to detail and accuracy here will go a long way.

[13]

B   Circle left 10 meters

[14]

H–K   Lengthen stride in canter
K   Working canter

[15]

FXH   Change rein; change of lead through trot at X

These three movements are the exact ones you just rode in the same order, but now they are repeated in the opposite direction. My previous directives apply, but remember to reverse the appropriate aids.

[16]

C   Working trot
MXK   Medium trot
K   Working trot

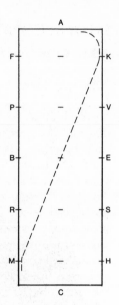

As you complete the previous movement, ride deeply into the corner after H in a working canter, then apply half-halts to prepare the horse for a downward transition to trot which occurs at C, right in front of the judge. Use the few steps of trot work you have from C to M to get the horse light in your hands and working off his hind end. The lighter, more cadenced, and balanced the horse is on the short side, the more length of stride he will show in the medium trot across the diagonal. Once again, bring him back to a working trot at K.

[17]

A Down center line
X Halt. Salute.

You should have ridden into the corner after K as though you were on a 10-meter circle, straightened the horse out on the short side, and again ridden the same 10-meter bend as you turned down the center line at A. Follow a straight line down to X, where you halt and salute as in previous tests.

AHSA SECOND LEVEL TEST 2

[1]

A Enter collected trot
X Halt. Salute. Proceed collected trot
C Track left

The rider is preparing to enter the arena in the collected trot, which is shorter and higher than the working trot.

Here the pattern of entry is the same as in previous tests, but the gait is different. Instead of starting with the working trot, this test — and the next four that follow — call for the horse to enter the arena at the collected trot.

A collected gait should show more engagement and balance, a better cadence, and an elevated stride which is not as long as in the working trot. The horse has to be worked into this gait because it takes a considerable degree of muscular development to achieve collection.

The horse's head should be approaching the vertical, with the highest point of the horse at the poll — not the fourth vertebra, as we often see. If he is properly moving from behind, the horse will feel very light in your hands and will have a period of suspension in his gait (cadence), which makes him move in an elegant manner.

Although the halt transition is the major factor for scoring this movement, the quality of your collected trot will influence the judge's impression as well. If you enter in a working trot, you will start off with fewer points than you would have been given for a collected trot. The judge's remark on your test sheet will likely read, "insufficiently collected," which is at best a 4.

As you move down the center line at collected trot from the halt, prepare the horse with half-halts and gentle leg aids for the right turn at C. Since you are in the collected trot, you have even more control over the horse's stride than before, because he is taking more steps as he covers the same distance. Therefore, you should be able to ride deeper into the corners as you turn off the center line and again as you turn up the long side.

[2]

E Turn left
B Turn right

In order to place the horse correctly on the E–B line, you have to start your first turn before you reach the letter E. Ride a straight line across the middle of the arena, and again begin to turn before you reach B.

Since this movement presents your horse sideways to the judge, he will look to see how much collection you have achieved. As you ride by, the judge can readily see whether the horse is on the bit and light in your hands, and whether he is moving with the higher degree of engagement expected in the collected trot. The principal part of this movement is riding from E to B, so it is scored mainly on the quality of the collected trot.

[3]

A Down center line
X Circle right 10 meters
X Circle left 10 meters
C Turn left

Here you turn down the center line and ride a figure eight, first to the right and then to the left. Think of this movement as two circles that touch at X (see diagram), as that is how it will be judged. The same principles apply here as for your 10-meter circles in previous tests.

The point where your circles meet (the middle of the figure eight, at X) should bisect the B–E line. Each circle places the horse five meters to either side of that line (towards the far ends of the arena — see diagram). Since the test calls for a full 10-meter circle, you must make your first one reach all the way out to B. As you come to the center of the figure eight, you should be on the A–C line for about one horse's length. Then change the bend of the horse to the left just after X, keeping the same rhythm as you make the next circle out to E. After you return to X, continue down the center line towards the judge and turn left at C.

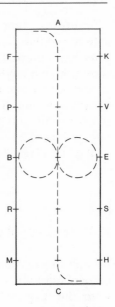

This is not an easy movement; it is found even in the FEI dressage tests and is not asked for before Second Level. It should be practiced at home, taking care not to go on a diagonal across the center of the figure eight, which would flatten out your circles. Riders have a tendency here to ride two egg-shaped circles, allowing the horse to pop a shoulder and not stay engaged — particularly inexcusable because you are in the collected trot.

[4]

HXF   Medium trot
F   Collected trot

You should have used your two turns after the last movement (at C and in the corner) to lighten and prepare the horse for the medium trot, which should begin right away at H. This is not a lengthening, where the judge might allow you a few strides to develop the gait. The medium trot should go from letter to letter, as it is ridden in Europe.

The horse is moving nicely in the collected trot, with the rider sitting properly and guiding him into the corner.

In this test, your medium trot ends at F. The judge should have been able to see two clear transitions into and out of the medium trot, because the collected work makes the transitions more distinct than they were from the working trot as in the previous test.

Notice that this medium trot — and all trot work from this point on — is done sitting. That means that with every stride, you should be able to drive with your seat and back to achieve a good medium trot. At this point, since the tests do not yet call for an extended trot, you may as well go for all the length of stride you can in the medium trot.

[5]

K–E Shoulder-in right

Be sure to use your corners right after the medium trot, especially the corner before the letter K, so that you are not starting the shoulder-in from the turn. Make the turn beforehand, straighten the horse out briefly on the long side, and *then* bring his front end one step off the rail for the shoulder-in. If you ride your shoulder-in directly out of the bend in the corner, you will lose points.

Although the shoulder-in was introduced in First Level Test 4, this is the first time you are asked to ride it from a straight line. Before, the shoulder-in was ridden directly out of a 10-meter circle, where the proper bend was already established. Here you have to think about riding the horse onto three tracks.

Use an active inside leg at the girth to drive the horse ahead. Begin the movement as though you were going to make a turn off the track. As the horse comes off the rail about one horse's width, apply your inside (right) leg and keep the same bend that you established to initiate the turn. The outside (left) rein becomes important because riders have a tendency here to pull the right rein too much, which causes the horse to overbend in the head and neck without bending through the body. Remember that the horse should be crossing over in front and going straight behind, so you gain a partial collection out of this movement.

This is an easy movement for the judge to evaluate, because he can see whether the horse is on three tracks and whether he is moving at the correct angle (see photo, p. 83). Be sure to keep a consistent angle all the way from K to E, or you will lose points.

[6]

E Circle right 10 meters

All the considerations given to our previous 10-meter circles apply here, but you may feel that this one is a bit of a breather because it comes between two difficult lateral movements. After you have gone from a shoulder-in into this circle, you have to go immediately into a travers in the next movement. Use this circle to prepare the horse, getting him as light and engaged as possible.

[7]

E–H Travers right

As you come off the circle, slide your left leg behind the girth to move the haunches in one horse's width as you bend the horse's head to the right. Ride the travers as directed in the previous test at this level (p. 91), then straighten the horse out at H and ride into the corner.

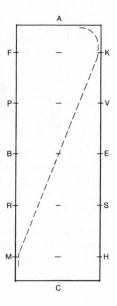

Crossing the diagonal in the medium trot, which this horse executes with the proper elevation and length of stride.

[8]

MXK Medium trot
K   Collected trot

[9]

F–B Shoulder-in left

[10]

B Circle left 10 meters

[11]

B–M Travers left

These four movements mirror the previous four movements, on the opposite hand. Ride them the same way you did the others, improving each one whenever possible to show the judge you are an alert and thinking rider. These movements are physically and mentally demanding for the horse. Since they come in the middle of a very long, 20-movement test, be prepared to drive the horse (and yourself!) if you feel either one of you tiring or losing concentration.

[12]

C Halt. Rein back 3–4 steps, proceed working walk

Drive the horse into a square, balanced halt at C, without allowing his head to come up. Hold the halt long enough to assure the judge that you have a halt. Sometimes horses arrive at C and immediately start to back, without first establishing the halt.

After the halt, ask the horse to take three or four steps backward by driving with your seat and closing your hands on the reins. The horse should remain on the bit, although some have a tendency to either come above it or to overflex and come way behind the bit. Either is undesirable.

The horse's body should be straight as he backs smoothly by diagonals, not dragging his feet or moving in a piecemeal fashion. Guide him backwards for three or four steps and then drive him forward into the walk so that he doesn't halt or square up after the last step backward.

[13]

HXK Medium walk

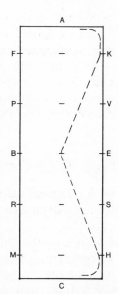

This is a new movement, which requires you to ride from H to the center of the arena at X, and then back out to K, forming a wide "V." You are in the medium walk, which is midway between the working and extended walks. The judge will be evaluating the extent of your horse's overstride, but he only has a good view for the first few strides after you leave H. The best advice here is to "go for it" right away, asking for as much length of stride as possible as soon as you make the turn off the long side and head towards X.

Let your horse reach out with his neck as he strides confidently forward, but don't let him get carried away with the forward motion and start jigging. As you approach X, begin to prepare the horse for a smooth turn back toward K. If a rider is going to make a mistake during this test, it usually comes here, when he or she forgets to turn at X and keeps riding across the diagonal. A dressage-savvy horse also may tend to anticipate a walk directly across the diagonal. It is your job to tell him otherwise.

[14]

K Working walk
A Collected canter, left lead
B Circle left 10 meters

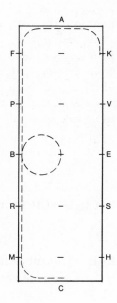

A horse at this level should be sufficiently balanced and engaged to move directly from the walk into the collected canter, with no trot steps in the transition. This is the first time the tests call for the collected canter, which requires the horse to have a higher topline, with his head approaching the vertical. The horse maintains a controlled canter tempo, but he shortens through the body and elevates his stride. The overall picture is rounder and lighter than the working canter.

When you move into the 10-meter circle here, you may find it easier to ride in a collected canter than it was in the working canter. In collected canter the horse should be lighter, more balanced, and in hand, enabling him to make a more precise 10-meter circle.

Make the circle come off the track at B without letting the horse pop a shoulder, come clear to X, bisecting the B–E line, and then come back to the track. The horse's body should be parallel to the long side when you come around to B.

[15]

H–K Medium canter
K Collected canter

This is a coefficient movement, where you can make some points by applying yourself (and your seat). The horse should really move out on the long side, showing a ground-covering medium canter from H to K, where there should be an obvious transition back into the collected canter.

[16]

FXH Change rein, change of lead through the trot at X

Ride into the corners after the previous movement to set up the turn onto the diagonal. Head straight from F to H, keeping the horse straight as he takes a few trot steps at X and then picks up the collected canter again, on the right lead. A horse who can perform a collected canter is likely to have been working at flying changes of lead, so he may anticipate one here at X. Make your aids very definite and keep your seat and legs quiet, so as not to confuse the horse.

[17]

B Circle right 10 meters

[18]

K–H Medium canter
H Collected canter

[19]

MXK Change rein, change of lead through trot at X

This series of movements repeats those from the last part of movement #14 through #16, but on the opposite rein. The crux of the matter comes in movement #18, where you should show a transition into and out of the medium canter. If anything, overdo it. This is a coefficient movement, but few riders take advantage of this opportunity to improve their score, for fear they won't be able to get the horse back at the end of the long side.

The key to getting around that problem lies in schooling. One of the most effective exercises I use for the medium canter begins with a 10-meter circle at K. As you come off the 10-meter circle, lengthen the horse out as much as possible, then ride another 10-meter circle at H to collect the horse. After you've done this several times and the horse is obedient, you can take the circles out and try to ride the medium trot with the same control.

When you make the downward transition back to collected canter at the end of the long side, keep your canter aids firm to prevent the horse from breaking into a trot, a common fault here. The change of lead across the diagonal rides the same as it did in movement #16 of this test.

[20]

F **Collected trot**
B **Turn left**
X **Turn right**
G **Halt. Salute.**

Use the corner to prepare for the transition from collected canter to collected trot at F. The tendency here is for the horse to make the transition, drift toward the center of the arena and then come back onto the track. Be sure you make the transition absolutely straight on the long side.

Make the turn at B so that you are on the B–E line, riding into a smooth turn onto the center line at X. Drive the horse forward towards the judge into a square halt at G.

Surprise! Although it does not have the traditional finale down the center line from A, the test is over.

AHSA SECOND LEVEL TEST 3

[1]

A Enter collected trot
X Halt. Salute. Proceed collected trot
C Track right

Your entry here is the same as in the previous test, but at C you track to the right. Since the test calls for you to enter at the collected trot, be sure to establish that gait before you make your turn down the center line. If you enter in a working trot and then collect the horse, you will lose points.

A horse at this level is expected to enter absolutely straight and to move without faltering from trot to halt at X. The horse's frame during the halt should remain as round as it was in the collected trot.

[2]

M–B Shoulder-in right
B   Turn right

Turn to the right at C, urging the horse to curve around your leg as though he were on a 10-meter circle. Straighten him out on the short side as you ride by the judge, and then drive him deeply into the next corner. Use half-halts through the turns so that you can go into the shoulder-in without the horse's head coming up as you put your inside leg on him to get the bend in his body. The horse should stay softly on the bit and engaged in the collected trot.

The transition into the shoulder-in is important. You must assume the angle that establishes the three-track movement immediately at M, and maintain that angle (in the same collection and frame) all the way to B. So often, judges witness the following: The horse comes above the bit as he takes his first steps into the shoulder-in. The rider works him back onto the bit halfway into the movement, but then the horse falls onto his shoulder as the rider overbends him in the neck.

Remember, the neck should only be bent sufficiently to get a slight curve from the horse's ear to his tail. If the horse is bent properly, he will be in the correct angle to ride smoothly into the right turn at B, as you guide him off the track and across the center of the arena.

[3]

E   Turn left
E–K Shoulder-in left

As in the previous movement, the rider should use the initial turn to lighten the horse with half-halts. Prepare him so that when you come off the turn, you smoothly continue the bend directly into the shoulder-in. The horse should be crossing over with his front legs and moving straight ahead with his hind legs as he maintains a consistent bend through his entire body.

When you reach K, straighten the horse out for the last few strides on the long side. Ride into your next corner as though it were a 10-meter circle.

[4]

FXH Medium trot
H   Collected trot

The lighter you can make the horse and the more you can engage him on the short side before coming to F, the more medium trot you will be able to achieve. Be sure your medium trot starts right at the letter F, not two or three strides into the diagonal, and continues all the way to H.

Ask for as much medium trot as you can get, keeping the horse in hand with his head a little higher than in a lengthening. Continue to ask the horse with your seat and legs in each stride across the diagonal, without driving so hard that he breaks into a canter. If you have the horse on the bit and engaged, he should accept your legs and extend his stride.

Of course, you cannot ask for what isn't there, so you should have already developed the medium trot during your schooling sessions at home. One of my most effective training methods for this is done on a circle: Collect the horse with a little shoulder-in, ask him to extend for a few steps, then collect him back into the shoulder-in (all the while on the circle). Repeat the process several times before riding off the circle. The circle keeps the horse bent and increases the engagement already established by the shoulder-in.

[5]

C Halt. Rein back 3 or 4 steps, proceed at collected trot

You should have ridden the corner deeply, because you need space to line up and be straight for the halt at C. The judge expects a smooth yet immediate transition from collected trot to halt, not from trot to walk to halt as we so often see. The lighter you have been able to make the horse with half-halts, the better your chances of getting a square halt.

If you can feel a good, "leg on each corner" halt underneath you, sit there a moment and enjoy it. Make sure the judge can see a definite halt. Too many riders here rush into the halt and then immediately start the rein-back. Sometimes in the halt there's still a hint of forward impulsion, in which case you should let the horse stand until you feel him relax.

Vibrate your fingers gently to get the horse soft on the bit, and then with your legs, cause him to back three or four steps. You should practice this at home so there is no doubt in the horse's mind that your aids mean to back smoothly, willingly, and by diagonals. One of the best training methods for this requires a helper on the ground. As you make your halt and ask the horse to back, when the horse resists by raising his head, the ground person taps the whip lightly on the front legs, causing the horse to back. You may have to repeat this lesson quite a few times, but usually the horse will learn fairly quickly to halt and back without a lot of fuss.

Since backing is physically demanding and can be somewhat hard on the hocks, the horse should be strong enough to do collected work before you start to back. I don't like to see riders ask green horses to back. With good reason, the halt and rein-back is not called for until Second Level, when systematic training should have made the horse sufficiently strong.

In this movement, you go from three or four steps of backing without a halt, and flow directly into a collected trot. The horse should be straight, remaining in a nice round frame and on the bit. The tendency of many horses here is to halt or to square up before they move forward. The horse should take several steps backward and then swing forward in the diagonal position, which is how judges prefer to see the movement done. To achieve this, sit deep as the horse takes his last step backward and drive him forward into the collected trot. It requires quite a bit of stability and balance to do what appears to be a simple movement here, so any time used schooling for this at home is well spent.

[6]

MXK Medium trot
K   Collected trot

The rein-back in the previous movement helps engage the horse, which prepares him for the medium trot here. Use half-halts in the corner to lighten and collect the horse more. Remember, extension comes from collection. My previous directives for medium-to-collected trot transitions apply here.

[7]

A   Working walk
F–M–C Medium walk

The judge expects to see the horse go immediately from collected trot to working walk at A. If the horse became tense in the medium trot, he is likely to show his tenseness by lifting his head and coming above the bit, or by becoming irregular at the walk and doing a bit of pacing. To avoid this, the transition at A must be done flowingly, which is impossible if a tense rider transmits his feelings to a horse that is already tense. It takes finesse to make this transition properly.

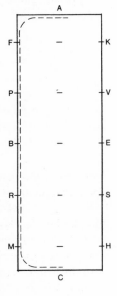

Although the horse is reaching forward into the medium walk, the reins are too slack. The rider needs to bring the horse together more.

After you make the corner, drive the horse into a medium walk at F, maintaining that gait all the way down the long side and around the track to C. Since there is no extended walk for comparison at this level, the rider should ask for as much overstep as he can get in the medium walk. It is not easy to keep the horse reaching out all the way from F to C, so the rider will have to work for his points. The horse must stay in a rhymthic four-beat gait, with his neck slightly above where it would be in a lengthened or extended walk.

This is a difficult movement for the judge to score because he cannot see the overstep until the horse is almost at M. This portion of the test unfortunately asks the judge to evaluate things he can only see at the very end. Be sure to "keep your foot on the gas pedal" so that your horse doesn't shorten his gait at the end of the long side, when the judge will be hoping to see something to score you on.

[8]

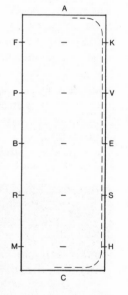

C   **Collected canter, left lead**
H–K   **Medium canter**
K   **Collected canter**

The first transition here is at C, directly in front of the judge. The horse must go from walk to canter with no trot steps. His canter must be engaged and collected, with his head approaching the vertical. Make sure he is straight when you ride him into the corner, and use the corner so he comes out of it straight.

At H, which is six meters in from the corner (see diagram), the horse must be absolutely straight and parallel to the long side as he makes the transition to medium canter. Lengthen the horse out into a medium canter right away. Most riders do little to show a difference between collected and medium canter. Since this is a coefficient movement, they are throwing away double points.

When you reach K, it is extremely important to show a transition from the medium canter to the collected canter. Keep the horse straight as he makes the transition and make sure he doesn't switch leads behind, which many have a tendency to do here. Lighten and balance the horse as quickly as possible after K to prepare for the next movement.

[9]

A–L Half circle, 18 meters
L   Simple change of lead, proceed to V
V   Turn right

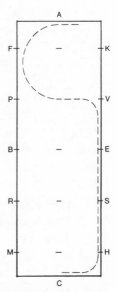

This precision exercise, the 18-meter half-circle, comes out two meters from the edge of the arena, which is just at the V–P line. In order to ride this movement accurately, you should trace it out at home so you know where 18 meters comes (see diagram). This is a new movement in the tests, incorporating a new distance and a new idea.

While you are striving to ride the figure accurately, don't forget to ride the horse. Keep him bent to the inside, moving properly in the collected canter and tracking his front footfalls with his hind. At the same time, you want to make the horse light to prepare for the simple change of lead as you cross the center line.

This is the first time the tests call for a simple change, instead of our previous change of lead through the trot. The simple change is made from collected canter to two or three steps of walk — not trot — and then into the other canter lead. What judges often see here is two or three steps of trot — as the horse runs through the rider's hands with his head in the air — then a step or two of walk, perhaps followed by a brief halt, and back into the canter. This, of course, will be scored down severely.

You need to work on this movement at home, because it is not as easy as it looks and it does carry a coefficient score. To execute it properly, the horse goes from canter to walk, which requires a considerable degree of collection and lightness in front. Then the horse must actually walk (not trot or pace), then move smoothly into the right-lead canter from the collected walk and turn back onto the track at V.

[10]

M–F Medium canter
F   Collected canter

From the previous movement, you follow the long side and come across the end, a distance you should use to lighten the horse for the medium canter at M. This is another coefficient movement in which you should show two transitions. The more collected you can get the horse before you start, the more transition you will be able to show. Exaggerate, if anything, the transitions into and out of the medium canter. If you make the effort here, you will earn the points. In Europe, you see riders really move the horse out into the medium canter, with precision, exactly from letter to letter. That is how it should be ridden in this country, as well.

[11]

A–L **Half-circle 18 meters**
L **Simple change of lead, proceed to P**
P **Turn left**

[12]

H–K **Medium canter**
K **Collected canter**

These movements repeat the previous two in this test (#9 and #10), on the opposite hand. The rider may have to work even harder this time, since it is almost the end of the test and the horse may be tiring.

[13]

A **Down center line**
L **Collected trot**
X **Halt. Salute**

As you turn at A to make your final halt and salute, the horse is in the collected canter for the first time on the center line. You proceed in the collected canter to L, which is 18 meters from the short end of the arena, on the center line between P and V. At L, you drive the horse down to a collected trot and proceed another 12 meters straight ahead to X, where you halt and salute.

AHSA SECOND LEVEL TEST 4

[1]

A Enter collected trot
X Halt. Salute. Proceed collected trot
C Track left

This is the same entry as in the previous two tests at this level. In this test, you turn left at C.

[2]

H–E Shoulder-in left

After C, be sure to ride deep into the corner so that the horse will be straight before you establish the shoulder-in at H. Usually the beginning of the shoulder-in is the difficult part because the horse may tend to resist and bring his head up. To avoid this, prepare him with half-halts in the corner.

Remember, this is an outside rein, inside leg movement. My previous directives on the shoulder-in apply: keep the horse on the bit, properly bent, and moving at a consistent 30-degree angle. The horse should be in the same collected stride he had while he made the turn on the short side. Do not let his tempo slow down, or the judge will mark you down for losing the rhythm.

[3]

E Circle left 10 meters

As you ride into this movement from the shoulder-in, the horse is already in the correct position for the 10-meter circle. Guide him smoothly off the rail and into the circle, making it round, not oval or lopsided. Too many times a rider will start the circle too soon or too late, which in either case results in an inaccurate circle. Remember, the judge expects you to ride this as a precision movement, keeping the horse in rhythm, on the bit, engaged, and in balance. It is important to make your circle bisect the B–E line, in the interests of accuracy and of setting yourself up properly to ride into the next movement.

[4]

E–K Travers left

As you come off the previous circle, you are automatically in the correct position to go into the travers (also called a haunches-in). The travers, which is in effect a half-pass on a straight line, is usually easier than the shoulder-in.

Because of the placement of this movement in the test and the judge's position at C, this movement is a difficult one for the judge to score. The rider's body blocks the judge's view of the horse's head carriage, so he will not know whether your horse is on the bit or whether his neck is bent to the inside. The judge can, however, tell whether the overall bend is correct and whether the horse is bent through the entire body.

Here again, it is important to keep the proper angle for the travers. Maintain rhythm and impulsion as you guide the horse on three tracks all the way from E to K and then straighten him out. Ride into the corner deeply and use the short side to set the horse up for the next movement.

[5]

FXH Medium trot
H   Collected trot

On the short side, you should have lightened the horse with half-halts, keeping his head up and driving him under from behind to prepare for the medium trot across the diagonal. Be sure to ride a straight line from F to H, showing a definite transition down to collected trot at H.

[6]

M–B Shoulder-in right

[7]

B Circle right 10 meters

[8]

B–F Travers right

[9]

KXM Medium trot
M   Collected trot

These four movements repeat the four we just rode, but, of course, on the opposite rein. The same considerations apply.

[10]

C Halt. Rein back 4 steps, proceed at medium walk

Ride into the corner after M, so you can have a straight approach to C, where you will halt so that your body is even with the letter C. If you get a good halt, sit briefly and enjoy it, allowing the horse to relax before you ask him to back.

This is the first test that specifically requires four backward steps, not "three or four" as in earlier tests at this level. Keeping the horse on the bit, use your seat and legs to ask the horse to back by diagonals. The judge wants the horse to lift his legs as he backs in a nice long stride. Too many horses stiffen here and drag their legs, just plowing through the rein-back.

Remember to count your steps backwards. The horse should go one-two-three-four-forward, without halting on the fourth step or squaring up. He should go directly from the diagonal position of his fourth step into the medium walk right away. Since the judge is sitting right there beside you, he is going to look immediately for overstep and regularity in the medium walk. If the horse is tense here and resisting through his back, you might get some irregularity or pacing instead of a pure four-beat marching tempo.

[11]

HXF Medium walk
F   Working walk

Here you cross the diagonal in the medium walk, which you have already established at C. Show as much overstride as possible right away, because the judge won't really be able to see how the horse is tracking after you pass X. Make an accurate, straight line across the diagonal.

As you approach F you need to concentrate on the transition to the working walk, which is midway between a collected walk and a medium walk. Start to use half-halts as you approach F to collect the horse. He should come more into your hand and his stride should shorten somewhat as he moves from the reaching strides of the medium walk into the working walk.

[12]

Between K & V Half-turn on haunches right

[13]

Between F & P Half-turn on haunches left

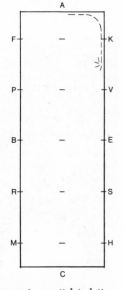

These are coefficient movements, executed first to the right and then to the left. The turn on the haunches is much the same movement as the pirouette (which is introduced at Third Level), but the difference is in degree. While the pirouette absolutely requires that the horse keep his hind end on the track, the horse is allowed to "gain a little ground" or come off the track slightly in the turn on the haunches. The front end of the horse must pivot — or pirouette — around the hind end of the horse while he maintains the walk tempo.

One of the best ways to work into this movement is to "think" a little shoulder-in, because that gives you some of the collection you will need and helps put the horse in the correct position for the turn on the haunches. Half-halts are appropriate here to alert the horse that a change is coming and to lighten him in front. If he is heavy on your hands, you will have trouble when you ask him for the turn on the haunches.

The sequence of steps for the half-turn on the haunches: The horse takes a step off the rail (first photo), maintaining the walk rhythm (second photo), as he turns and comes back onto the rail in the opposite direction (third photo).

Since the rider controls the front end of the horse with the reins, you guide him into movement #12 by lifting the horse to the right with a strong outside rein. This rein, in an indirect manner, ties the horse's neck and shoulder together, allowing you to lift the entire front end of the horse around his hind end. The outside rein is also important in keeping the horse from overbending in his neck. At the same time, your inside rein works to keep the horse's head to the inside so that it is leading, not going behind the movement.

Emphasize the inside leg on the girth to keep the horse from losing rhythm or from "getting stuck," which happens when the inside hind leg doesn't stay in the walk sequence and "drills a hole in the ground." From the judge's point of view, this is insufficient (earning at best a mark of 4) because the horse is irregular and is not maintaining the walk tempo as required.

That is the difficult part of this movement — keeping the horse from burying his inside hind leg and from shifting out of the walk rhythm. He must lift his inside hind leg up and down in the walk tempo, staying as close to the track as possible, as his front legs cross (the outside reaching over the inside — see third photo on p. 119). The entire movement should appear light, flexible, supple, and rhythmical.

Although horses tend to learn the turn on the haunches rather readily, it is the rider's job to practice enough so the horse understands what he has to do in this part of the test. It is not something that comes naturally to a horse.

Be sure to guide the horse all the way around the half-turn, so that you end up back on the track. Too many times judges see horses (especially in the last stride) step out of the turn, which brings them further from the track and ends the movement off the track. When your turn is completed, keep the horse's haunches in place on the track with your outside leg behind the girth as you continue in the walk.

[14]

A Collected canter right lead
E Circle right 10 meters

The judge can see your transition at A from walk to collected canter in profile, so it should be executed smoothly and quietly, with the horse engaged and on the bit. The horse should flow into the upward transition, with no trot steps in between. He should be in the collected canter from his first stride, not heavy on the forehand at first and then working into collection.

Ride into the corner and straighten the horse out on the long side to set him up for the 10-meter circle at E. Lighten the horse with half-halts as you approach E, and use your right rein when you come off the track to keep the horse from popping a shoulder. The outside rein is important here as well, for the rider must keep the horse together by coordinating the use of both reins and by using his leg aids to keep the horse bent through the body and tracking up.

Remember to make your circle bisect the B–E line, coming clear out to X so that you are making a full 10-meter circle. The judge is sitting on the C–A line, so he or she will look to see whether your circle is round and how far it comes out. The tendency for most riders here is to make the circle too large. It takes a considerable degree of collection for a horse to do a proper 10-meter circle at the canter.

[15]

E Simple change of lead;
proceed to M in counter-lead

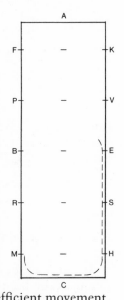

The simple change, by definition, is a transition from canter to a few walk steps and back into the canter on the other lead. It is not canter-trot-walk-canter, and it requires more collection than the change of lead through the trot, which is normally done across the diagonal.

Here you are better off because the change is done on a circle, where it is easier for the horse to drop from canter to walk than it would be on a straight line. When you have the walk at E, take a few steps and make sure the horse is straight when you ask him for the canter. During the transition, the horse should not halt or come off the track. He should flow into the counter-canter, which is a coefficient movement.

The counter-canter is a strenuous gymnastic exercise for the horse. His initial tendency may be to pull a little and stiffen, or perhaps to change leads in front and become disunited. The rider must sit quietly to keep the horse together and in balance, and to make him understand that you want a counter lead. Keep your aids steady and do not shift your weight, or the horse may think you want a flying change. (As we get into the upper-level movements it becomes more and more critical not to confuse the horse, because one aid may be interpreted several

The horse has made the simple change of lead at E and is proceeding toward M in the counter-canter, although he doesn't look completely pleased about it. Since he is somewhat stiff and resistant here, the score for this movement will be lower.

different ways, depending upon how the rider coordinates it with other aids.) The horse is bent slightly to the outside as you continue around the arena in the collected canter.

[16]

MXK Change rein; no change of lead

At M you cross the diagonal in the collected canter, which will put you automatically back in the true canter when you reach K. Sit quietly across the diagonal, still keeping your aids steady. If you feel the horse start to slow down near X in anticipation of a flying change, drive him forward with your seat and back but do not change the pressure or position of your legs.

As you ride the medium canter down the long side, begin to prepare at B for a downward transition to collected canter at the next letter, R.

[17]

F–R Medium canter
R   Collected canter

This medium canter sequence is different than previously, because here you make the transition back to collected canter at R (see diagram). The horse is probably somewhat attuned to making the transition at M as before, so it is important for the rider to wake him up with half-halts before he reaches the letter R (see photo). If you make this transition precise and accurate at the letter it will certainly impress the judge. Very seldom do we see a good transition from medium to collected canter done right at the R and with engagement.

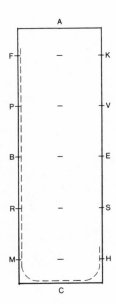

[18]

E Circle left 10 meters

[19]

E Simple change of lead; proceed to F in counter-lead

[20]

FXH Change rein; no change of lead

[21]

M–P Medium canter
P   Collected canter

This sequence mirrors, on the opposite hand, the same movements we just rode in #14–#17. Ride this sequence the same way, but with a little more gusto, because the horse may be tiring in these final movements of a very long and demanding test. Be sure to get the horse back from the medium to the collected canter at P, because your next transition comes up very quickly.

[22]

F Collected trot
A Down center line
G Halt. Salute.

You need to collect and balance the horse right away in the previous canter transition at P, in order to make this transition down to the collected trot at F. It takes a thinking and skillful rider to execute both of these transitions flowingly such a short distance apart.

The transition at F is important because it is where you will prepare the horse for his last ride down the center line, where you will make your final impression on the judge. Be straight as you trot down the center line from A, which should be easier and more accurate to ride in collection than it was in earlier tests in the working trot.

Ride all the way down to G for your salute, which occurs between M and H. If you are unsure of where G really is, as a number of riders appear to be here, look for the cross-mark on the center line.

4. Third Level

The previous test should have helped you bridge the gap to Third Level. Second Level Test 4 contains several movements that were Third Level movements under the 1979 tests, such as the 10-meter circle to the change of lead with counter-canter. Your horse will need even more strength and balance to perform these Third Level movements, which require a higher degree of collection: pirouettes, the four-loop serpentine, and eight-meter circles. The extended trot, which rounds out your work at all the gaits, takes more engagement than the medium trot.

AHSA THIRD LEVEL TEST 1

[1]

A Enter collected trot
X Halt. Salute. Proceed collected trot
C Track right

The horse should be in a light collected trot as you come into the arena. Drive him straight ahead to X, where he should halt in balance and on the bit. Establish a square halt and make a dramatic salute. Regain your rein contact, soften the horse, and ask him to move absolutely straight ahead into the collected trot. Keep your legs evenly on his sides to keep him straight on the center line until you approach C, where he should make a smooth turn to the right.

[2]

MXK Medium trot
K   Collected trot

Prepare for the medium trot on the short side with half-halts. The lighter and more engaged you get the horse, the more medium trot he will give you. Be sure to establish the medium trot right away at M. Ride straight across the diagonal and emphasize the transition back to the collected trot precisely at K.

[3]

A Down center line
X Circle left 8 meters

Begin your turn just before A so that you do not overshoot the center line. At X, you make an eight-meter circle, the first time the tests have called for a circle this size. In this case, the circle comes two meters in from E (see diagram), which requires precision and balance.

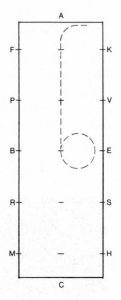

[4]

X–G Shoulder-in right
C   Turn right

Here is a new twist on a movement you are already familiar with: the shoulder-in. This test calls for you to ride the movement down the center line, which is more difficult than before because you don't have the side of the arena to guide you.

As you come out of the previous circle, everything is right to move smoothly into the shoulder-in. Ride as though you were going to continue the circle, establishing a uniform bend from ears to tail. Come one horse's width off the track and apply a strong inside leg to drive the horse straight ahead into the shoulder-in.

Common errors here are overbending the neck with an insufficient bend in the body, losing the rhythm, or the horse coming above the bit when you apply your inside leg. These are easy for the judge to spot, because he is sitting directly in front of you.

Straighten the horse on the center line at G and ride straight toward C, where you make a smooth, balanced turn to the left.

[5]

HXF Extended trot
F Collected trot

This is the first extended trot called for in the tests. You must prepare for it with half-halts on the short side. When you drive the horse into extension, the judge expects to see the horse lower his head and neck more than in the medium trot (see photo). Try to cover as much ground with as much engagement as possible, without interrupting the rhythm.

In the extended trot, which is a coefficient move-

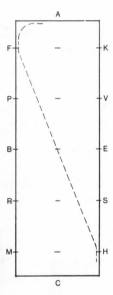

ment, you should go all out. In this country, the majority of riders don't ask for the ultimate because they don't have their horses sufficiently balanced and are afraid they may break into a canter. Cautious riding here is not going to earn you points.

At F, show a clean, clear, driving transition down to the collected trot. This transition should be even more obvious than it was from the medium-to-collected trot in movement #2 of this test.

[6]

A Down center line
X Circle right 8 meters

[7]

X–G Shoulder-in right
C   Turn right

[8]

MXK Medium trot
K   Collected trot

The first two movements here (#6 and #7) mirror movements #3 and #4 of this test. The third movement (#8) rides exactly the same as movement #2 of this test. At this point you have already ridden an extended trot, so be sure to show the judge a difference in your medium trot here.

[9]

A Halt. Rein back 4 steps, proceed collected walk

The key to the halt here is to have the horse light. A horse who is heavy in front is likely to plunge into the trot in a heavy manner. If you get a square, balanced halt, emphasize it by holding the halt a moment. When the horse is relaxed in the halt, pick him up and with your seat ask him to back by diagonals in as long a stride as possible. In the diagonal of the fourth step, drive the horse forward into the collected walk, taking care not to lose him off the bit or to disturb the rhythm.

[10]

FXH Extended walk
H   Collected walk

Ride your previous corner to prepare for this coefficient movement. Allow the horse to reach slightly down and out with his neck so that he can stretch his whole body into the extended walk, but don't lose contact with his mouth because this is not a free walk. His gait should be relaxed and rhythmical, showing as much overstride as possible. The rider may encourage more length of stride by applying alternate leg aids. The judge cannot see the amount of overstep until you reach X, so at that point be sure you have achieved your horse's maximum walk stride.

Be careful when you collect the horse at H. Oftentimes, horses who are somewhat tense when they are asked to collect here will do some jigging or short trot steps. This will lose you most of the points you have earned because the gait is irregular and is not the one specified in the test. You should work on the transition from extended to collected walk at home, because it is not as easy as it sounds and a poor mark here can drastically affect your overall score for the test.

In the extended walk, the horse lengthens his stride as much as possible.

[11]

Between M & R Half-pirouette right, proceed collected walk

[12]

Between H & S Half-pirouette left, proceed collected walk

This is the first time the tests call for the pirouette. It is to be performed between the two letters specified, and where you do it is immaterial. Some riders start it right away after the first letter, others wait until they are almost at the second letter, and still others do it in the middle.

The difference between the pirouette and the turn on the haunches is a matter of degree. In the pirouette, the horse must be more collected. He must keep his hind legs on the track, lifting his inside leg to keep the walk rhythm (which is the difficult part) as he pivots around in front. The outside front leg must reach over the inside, and the head must lead the movement.

If the horse "sticks" or "grounds" his inside hind leg, he is out of the walk tempo. Horses tend to do this if they are not supple and flexible enough behind because grounding the leg makes it easier for them. It is up to the rider to prevent this by keeping the forward movement with an inside leg on the girth. Keep your outside leg behind the girth so the haunch doesn't pivot, especially in the third or fourth step when the horse may want to shift sideways.

I find the pirouette comes easily to my horses because I introduce it when they are quite young. I never teach the turn on the forehand because it can cause complications later on. Horses like the turn on the forehand; once they learn it, many of them try to dance around their front end every time they halt. Your time is better spent schooling in the turn on the haunches and graduating into the pirouette.

[13]

C   Collected canter, right lead
M–F Medium canter
F   Collected canter

Here you must go directly from collected walk into collected canter, which is not a difficult transition if the horse is light and balanced. Intermediary trot steps here are inexcusable, as is the horse plunging into a strong canter. Instead, his hocks should be underneath him as he flows into the collected canter.

The more collection you attain here, the more medium canter you will get on the long side. Ride the corner deeply so the horse is straight when he begins the medium canter at M. Work for length of stride and pay attention to straightness, particularly when you ask the horse to collect at F. Often horses tend to bring their hind legs in at the end of this movement. To prevent this, keep the horse bent slightly to the inside, with your seat square and your inside leg on the horse's side.

[14]

E Circle right 10 meters
E Simple change of lead

Make sure your circle is round and a full 10 meters, coming all the way out to X, and that your horse is in the collected canter. Use half-halts to make the horse light so that when you come back to E, you can make the simple change of lead. Remember, a simple change means that you go from true canter to a few walk steps and then into the counter-canter. It is not as easy as it sounds, because the horse must be straight through the transition and cannot become agitated, as some do.

A nice bend, as the horse completes the 10-meter circle in the canter and approaches E. The rider is looking ahead to the letter, where she will ask for a simple change of lead.

[15]

C–A Serpentine of four loops, no change of lead

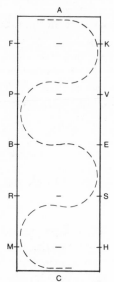

I consider this movement a little too difficult for Third Level because it contains four loops. Curiously, in Fourth Level, the serpentine only has three loops. Nonetheless, it is part of this test, so you must perfect it.

You start at C, where you are already in the counter-canter from the previous movement, and this time do not ride into the corner. Ride away from the track, making a nice smooth curve clear out to the edge of the arena, which puts you into the true canter as you cross the center line and make your second loop. The third loop is counter-canter and the fourth is again the true canter.

These loops must be evenly spaced so that they are absolutely symmetrical (see diagram). The difficulties are balance, accuracy, and maintaining the counter-canter, since the horse may try to change leads. This is quite a gymnastic exercise.

[16]

F–M Extended canter
M Collected canter

This is a coefficient movement, and the first time the tests have called for an extended canter. You should go all out here, as you did in the extended trot. Ask for as much length of stride as you can in control, so that the horse does not run off with you. Drive with your back and seat, keeping your inside leg on the girth and your outside leg slightly behind.

At M, show a definite transition back to the collected canter, taking care that the horse does not change leads behind or bring his haunches in when he collects.

[17]

E Circle left 10 meters
E Simple change of lead

[18]

A–C Serpentine of four loops, no change of lead

These two movements mirror those in movements #14 and #15 of this test. My same directives apply.

[19]

C   Collected trot
MXK Extended trot
K   Collected trot

At C, where you finish your serpentine, you go from collected canter to collected trot. Make the trot *collected*. The more you can lighten and collect your horse before the extension, the better. Use half-halts along that short distance you have on the short side to get the horse light, engaged, and balanced. Go clear from M to K in extension, keeping the same rhythm as your collected trot, and show another definite transition back to collection at K.

[20]

A Down center line
X Halt. Salute.

Use the corner after the last movement to set up your turn at A here so that you hit the center line precisely. Keep your leg pressure even so that the horse stays straight on the center line. Drive him forward to X, where you make a transition from collected trot to halt. Balance the halt and make your usual dramatic salute.

AHSA THIRD LEVEL TEST 2

[1]

A Enter collected trot
X Halt. Salute. Proceed collected trot
C Track left

[2]

HXF Medium trot
F   Collected trot

The first movement — the enter-halt-salute sequence — is the same as in previous tests. Make sure your horse is collected as he enters at A, stays straight down the center line, and is balanced in his halt at X.

Concentrate right away on collecting, balancing, and engaging your horse as you move off from X, because you only have a short distance before the medium trot at H. Ride into the corners and use half-halts on the two short turns to set up the medium trot. My previous directives on the medium trot-collected trot sequence apply.

[3]

K–X Half-pass right
X   Straight ahead
C   Turn right

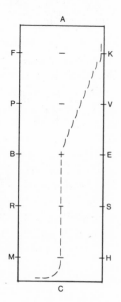

Here is the first time the tests have called for the half-pass. The half-pass is the outcome of the tests' logical progression from leg-yield to shoulder-in to travers. The best preparation for the half-pass is the shoulder-in. If you ride a slight shoulder-in until you reach K and then put your outside leg behind the girth, you will align the horse into a half-pass position.

The half-pass is exactly what its name implies: moving halfway (45 degrees) to the front and halfway to the side at the same time. In order to achieve this, you must get the haunches mobile,

In the half-pass, the horse's front and hind legs cross over. Notice the rider's distinct aids.

light, and crossing over. The rider's seat controls the horse's hind end. Your outside leg behind the girth pushes the haunches over (see photo), while your inside leg on the girth maintains the forward impulsion. The outside (indirect) rein unites the horse's front end and causes his front legs to cross over. The inside (direct) rein makes the horse's head lead slightly in the direction of the movement.

The judge wants to see the horse's head lead the movement as his body stays parallel to the long sides of the arena and his legs cross over, front and hind. From the judge's vantage point at C, he or she has a clear, head-on view of all these elements. The judge can easily see whether the horse is well-balanced, or so unbalanced that he wobbles and loses the angle, or whether the horse drags his hind legs because he is not sufficiently engaged, another common fault.

This is a coefficient movement, and when it is done flowingly it is a beautiful one. But remember that the scoring doesn't end at X. The judge will still be watching to see whether you bring the horse back into absolute straightness all the way from X to C (see diagram).

[4]

MXK Extended trot
K   Collected trot

[5]

F–X Half-pass left
X   Straight ahead
C   Turn left

[6]

E Turn left
X Halt; rein back 4 steps; proceed at collected trot
B Track right

For movements #4 and #5, refer to my previous directives for these movements on the opposite rein. For movement #6, begin your turn to the left slightly before you reach E, so that the horse ends up straight on the E–B line. Drive the horse to a square halt at X. The judge has a profile view of you here, so make sure your horse is balanced and on the bit as he makes a nice square halt.

Establish the halt and ask the horse to back by diagonals, lifting his feet in a marching tempo. He should take four distinct steps straight backward, without his head coming up or overflexing downward. This movement is more difficult than in previous tests, because here you are performing it in the middle of the arena, without the sides for guidance. In the diagonal of the fourth step, the horse must move confidently forward into the collected trot.

[7]

F   Collected walk
AKV Medium walk
VXR Extended walk
RMC Medium walk
C   Collected walk

Here comes the true test of your horse's walk gaits — and of your finesse as a rider. The judge expects to see five definite transitions here and a clear difference between the three types of walk strides. At the beginning of this movement, when you are way down at the far end of the arena, it is difficult for the judge to assess how much the horse oversteps, but he will get a general picture of the way the horse is moving.

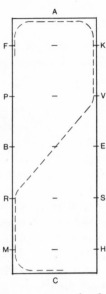

Remember that at F, the collected walk should have higher and shorter action than the medium or extended walk, with the hind foot replacing or coming slightly behind the front hoofprint. At A you must show a transition to the medium walk, with enough overstride for the judge to score you on, but not so much that he won't see any difference when you move into the extended walk across the short diagonal from V to R (see diagram). Go all out in the extended walk, showing as much overstep as your horse can achieve without breaking the gait. The judge has a profile view here, and he is close enough to assess the overstep. At R and C, where you are close to the judge, overemphasize the transitions back to the medium and collected walks, respectively.

[8]

Between H & S   Half-pirouette left,
proceed at collected walk

[9]

Between M & R Half-pirouette right,
proceed at collected walk

The pirouettes should be light and flowing, and executed in the four-beat walk rhythm. Re-read my directives for this movement in Third Level Test 1 (p. 130).

[10]

C   Collected canter left lead
H–K Medium canter
K   Collected canter

The first transition here, from collected walk to collected canter, is performed right in front of the judge. Make it flowing and establish the collection right away, so that you can show a transition to the medium canter at H. If you can "throw a little dirt" onto the judge's scorecard when your horse digs in at H, all to the good.

Drive the horse into a medium canter precisely from H to K, making sure that he stays straight, parallel to the long side. At K, where you bring the horse back into collection, keep your inside leg on him to bend him slightly to the inside, so that he does not bring his haunches to the inside of the track. If the horse does not stay straight during this transition, it is considered quite a serious fault and will be scored down accordingly.

[11]

F–M Extended canter
M   Collected canter

Your last movement was a transition from medium to collected canter, so here you must show an even more obvious transition between extension and collection. To score well, you must show the judge more length of stride in this extended canter than you did in the medium canter. At M, you must come back into collection right away in order to perform the next movement.

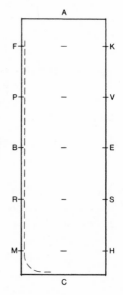

This horse is covering enough ground in the extended canter, but his open mouth is a sign of resistance — which will mean a lower score.

[12]

C Turn on center line
I–P Half-pass left

This is the first time the tests have called for a turn on the center line in the canter after an extension. If you do not have the horse completely in hand during the turn from M onto the short side, you are likely to overshoot the center line.

Here you ride the half-pass from I to P, which is a tighter half-pass than previously and is also the first time the half-pass is done in the canter. This movement is usually easier to ride in the canter because the horse is lighter and is generally more willing to move away from your leg. Horses seem to enjoy the canter half-pass, so they tend to cooperate here.

[13]

F Simple change of lead

[14]

K–H Medium canter
H Collected canter

The simple change here will be easier to perform if you have the horse light and engaged when you straighten him out at P. From there, you ride a transition from medium to collected canter, which you should be able to perform smoothly by now, without further directives.

[15]

M–F Extended canter
F   Collected canter

[16]

A   Down center line
L–R Half-pass right

[17]

M Simple change of lead

This sequence mirrors that in movements #11–#13 of this test (p. 138).

In the half-pass (here performed at the canter), the horse is looking in the direction of travel.

[18]

C   **Collected trot**
HXF **Extended trot**
F   **Collected trot**

There is not much distance between your true canter at M and the collected trot at C, so this is rather a difficult movement. Use your collected trot to balance the horse so that he can move immediately into an extended trot at H. The way to ride this is to collect, collect, collect on the short side, turn the corner, and at H sit deep for a driving extension all the way across the diagonal. At F, settle into the saddle, bring the horse back into your hands, and drive him down into a collected trot.

[19]

A Down center line
X Halt five seconds,
    proceed collected trot
G Halt. Salute.

Use the previous corner to set up your turn onto the center line at A. Ride straight to X, where you go directly into the halt and hold it for five full seconds. Most judges will count to themselves "one-two-three-four-five," but for some reason most riders do not seem to be able to count to five.

From the halt, move foward into the collected trot for a few strides until you reach G, where you halt and salute as usual.

AHSA THIRD LEVEL TEST 3

[1]

A Enter collected canter
X Halt. Salute. Proceed collected trot
C Track right

This begins with the normal entry and halt on the center line, but in this final test at Third Level (and in the following two at Fourth Level), the entry is ridden in the collected canter instead of the trot. The canter should be straight, three-beat, relaxed, engaged, and balanced as you approach X, where you go directly from canter to halt. Since there is more impulsion involved, this may be more difficult than our previous trot-to-halt transitions.

[2]

MXK Medium trot
K Collected trot

You should have used half-halts on the turns at C and M to prepare and lighten the horse for the medium trot across the diagonal. Be sure the diagonal is ridden straight, with precise transitions right at M and K.

[3]

A Down center line
X Circle left 8 meters

A circle of only eight meters, which was introduced in the first test at Third Level (p. 126), is physically demanding for the horse. As in the larger circles at lower levels, the inherent challenges of the figure remain: Make the figure accurate and round, keep the horse bent to the inside but without "falling in" on his inside shoulder, and maintain the collected trot rhythm throughout the entire circle. Your circle must bisect the B–E line and come two meters in from the edge of the arena (see diagram, p. 126). As you complete the eight-meter circle and return to X, you are correctly positioned for the next movement.

[4]

X–G Renvers left
C   Track left

Here the tests introduce another new movement: the renvers (haunches-out). This movement, which is really a half-pass on a straight line, requires the horse's head to be bent in the direction of movement. It is a three-track movement, with the horse's legs crossing over both in front and behind. You must maintain the proper bend and ride into the movement, without the horse changing his balance or coming off the bit. All the way from X to G, the horse must maintain the same rhythm and cadence. At G, you straighten the horse and ride directly toward the judge at C, where you turn to the left. This is a coefficient movement, which is performed right on the C–A line in front of the judge.

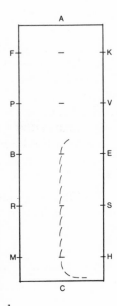

[5]

HXF Extended trot
F   Collected trot

The collection attained through the renvers should help prepare the horse for the extended trot here. Use the corners to further lighten and balance the horse so that when you ask for extension at H you achieve it right away. Keep the horse extending straight across the diagonal to F, where he should collect again.

[6]

A Down center line
X Circle right 8 meters

[7]

X–G Renvers right
C Track right

[8]

M–F Medium trot
F Collected trot

A renvers to the right, ridden on the center line towards the judge.

This sequence mirrors movements #3–#5, except that this time you end with a downward transition from the medium trot instead of the extended trot. Try for as much medium trot as you can get right away, because as you move down the long side away from the judge, he or she will be less able to observe the extent of your medium trot. Be sure to drive the horse into a collected trot at F and to line yourself up with the corner so the horse will be straight on the short side for the next movement.

[9]

A Halt; rein back four steps; proceed at collected walk

This is similar to our previous trot-to-halt transitions into the rein-back, but this time you move forward into the walk instead of the trot. When the horse is in the diagonal of his fourth step, apply a light leg aid to make him move forward into the collected walk (see photos). Don't be abrupt or too strong with your legs, or the horse may lurch forward into the trot, which will cause you to lose points.

The halt-and-rein-back sequence: First, bring the horse to a nice square halt. Next ask the horse to back by diagonals. In the diagonal of the fourth step, ask him to move forward (third photo).

[10]

K–S Extended walk
S–C Medium walk

In the first part of this movement — the extended walk — the horse's head should reach down and out, but without losing contact. The horse should show as much freedom of movement as possible, maintaining a four-beat walk tempo, with the hind foot overstepping the front print by a generous amount.

At S, you must show a transition from extended to medium walk. Do not slow the tempo, just shorten the stride slightly. There should be less overstep in the medium walk, with the action slightly higher than in the extended walk.

[11]

C	Collected walk
M	Turn right
Between G & H	Half-pirouette right

[12]

Between G & M Half-pirouette left

Ride the horse in the collected walk from C to M, where you turn to perform the half-pirouette between G and H. In this movement, the horse must pivot on his hind end, yet still maintain the walk tempo. The head leads, with a direct rein. The outside rein ties the shoulder and neck together. Your inside leg driving on the girth maintains the forward impulsion, and your outside leg behind the girth keeps the horse from stepping to the side behind and turning on his forehand. The difficult part is to keep the hind end in place, at the same time maintaining the walk rhythm.

[13]

G	Collected canter, left lead
H–K	Medium canter
K	Collected canter

[14]

**B Half-circle left 10 meters,
returning to the track at P,
proceed at counter-lead to A**

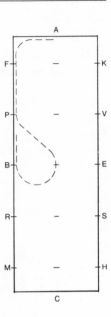

By now, you should be competent at the transitions between the collected and medium canters, so I will give no further directives for movement #13. To ride the next movement — the canter half-circle into the counter-lead — you guide the horse off the track just after he passes the letter B. Ride a smooth, engaged half-circle to X, where you turn and head back to the track at P (see diagram). This is a rather tight turn, so you must keep the horse engaged, balanced, and in rhythm. When you reach P, the horse is bent to the outside in the counter-canter, so keep your aids steady to avoid a change of lead.

[15]

A Circle right 20 meters with flying change on center line

Here is the first time the tests require a flying change of lead, which is a step up from the simple changes in earlier tests. The first half of this circle is done in the counter-lead you established in the previous movement. When you come to the center line you must reverse your aids to achieve a flying change to the true canter (see diagram, p. 149). To get a correct change (simultaneously in the front and rear), the rider must ask for it at the moment of suspension, bending the horse to the inside.

Common faults here occur when the horse bears on the rider's hands and refuses to change, changes just in front, or changes first in front and then changes behind a stride or two later. The judge will score you down in any of these instances, so if you feel resistance coming when you prepare for the change, apply a little extra persuasion with the whip or a spur.

In order to get a horse to the point where I am confident he will accept flying changes, I want to be almost 100 percent sure that he understands when I want him to take the left or right lead. I ascertain this by riding down the long side of the arena in this pattern: three strides on the right-lead canter, a few steps of collected walk, then three strides on the left-lead canter. I repeat this on the center line and then vary the pattern to see if the horse becomes confused. I might ask for two strides of right-lead canter, then walk, then three strides again on the right lead. Eventually I'll work the horse on a 20-meter circle, starting with the true canter to a few walk steps and into the counter-canter for the rest of the circle. The horse really has to agree that even though he is turning to the left, he is being directed to take the right lead. When the horse reaches this stage of understanding, performing the flying change is relatively simple if your timing is right.

The first time I ask the horse in training for a flying change, I begin on a 20-meter circle in the counter-canter. I ease the position of the horse's head from an outside bend to an inside bend and wait until I feel him relaxed and rhythmical. Then I apply the aids for the other lead vigorously, perhaps vibrating the whip so there is no confusion. If I get a correct flying change — as I do almost 100 percent of the time using this method — I stop the horse, pat him, and reward him.

[16]

K–H Extended canter
H   Collected canter

Here the horse is in the collected canter, finishing the last portion of this movement. Remember, you are still being judged for this movement until a new one begins at the next letter, B.

[17]

**B Half-circle right to M, returning to the
track at R. Proceed at counter-lead to C**

[18]

**C Circle left 20 meters with flying change
on center line**

Movement #16 does not require further directives.
Movements #17 and #18 repeat the sequence we
just rode in movements #14 and #15.

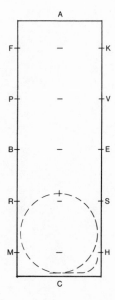

[19]

C   Collected trot
HXF Extended trot
F   Collected trot

As you complete your previous circle at C, you have a transition from
collected canter to collected trot. Make it flow, and use half-halts on
the short side so that the horse will be ready to extend right away at H.
Ride a straight diagonal and drive the horse into a collected trot at F.

[20]

A Down center line
X Halt. Salute.

No surprises here. Since there are no supplementary movements here
as in some of the earlier tests, be sure you attain a precise halt for the
judge to score you on.

5. Fourth Level

The Fourth Level horse is expected to perform many of the same movements as he did in Third Level, but now the transitions are more frequent. These tests are extremely exacting and lengthy, with 26 movements each (six more than at Third Level). Not only do you have to ride intricate movements with precision, but you may have to work harder to maintain impulsion if your horse tires in the latter half of these tests.

The Fourth Level tests are designed to be difficult because they represent the highest national (non-FEI) level of dressage in this country. Once you are scoring consistently in the 60's in these tests, you are ready to ride the tests at the international (FEI) levels — and at that point you won't be referring to a handbook for your knowledge.

AHSA FOURTH LEVEL TEST 1

[1]

A Enter collected canter
X Halt. Salute. Proceed collected trot
C Track right

This is the same entry we just rode in Third Level Test 3, but because this test is at a higher level, the judge will expect to see an even more solid entry. Since this first movement does not specify the canter lead on the center line (as is required later in the test), you may enter on either the left or right lead. I strongly suggest you choose your horse's "good" side, because as you enter the arena you are largely being judged on your horse's canter. The judge wants it to be straight, balanced, rhythmical, and engaged, so you can drive the horse into a square halt at X. Don't forget to ride the horse in collection throughout this movement and the next three that follow.

[2]

M–B Shoulder-in right

At this level your horse's shoulder-in should be well established. Ride him deep into the previous corner, so that he is straight when he starts down the long side. At M, bring his front end slightly off the track, taking care to keep him on the bit. Any form of resistance in the shoulder-in (which usually comes from the front end, most often with the horse hollowing his back and coming above the bit) will be glaringly evident to the judge in this movement. Avoid this by driving with your inside leg and guiding the horse's head gently away from the direction of movement (see photo). Remember, his front legs must cross over while his hind legs move straight ahead, forming three distinct tracks. The judge wants the horse to show suppleness and balance, and to maintain the same angle all the way from M to B.

The proper angle in the shoulder-in to the right, with the horse bent correctly through the entire body. Frank Daigle, Darlene Sordillo's trainer, is shown here practicing the movement on the opposite side of the arena, so the horse will not always anticipate it at M.

[3]

B Circle right 8 meters

The eight-meter circle was introduced in the Third Level tests (p. 126), but it was only called for a total of four times (twice in each direction).

It occurs in the third movement of this test, and again in the first two FEI tests (Prix St. Georges and Intermediaire 1). So if you are aspiring toward the FEI levels of international dressage, it is to your benefit to master the nuances of the eight-meter circle, which is ridden in the collected trot.

Because of its placement in this test, the circle must bisect the B–E line. Keep your inner leg on the girth to maintain the impulsion, because your horse's gait is also being judged here. Keep your outside leg slightly behind the girth, to hold the haunches so that they don't swing out. If the horse is correctly bent from ear to tail, his hind legs will follow in the tracks made by his front legs on the circle. Otherwise, the judge will mark you down for "losing the haunches."

[4]

B–D Half-pass right
A   Track right

Establishing the proper bend in the previous circle will pay off here, because as you finish the circle you ride immediately into a half-pass right. If the horse was round in the eight-meter circle, it will be relatively easy to establish the half-pass here, because the angle is almost the same. The horse's head should already be to the inside, and he should be balanced and engaged. Keep the horse moving forward with your inside leg on the girth and position your outside leg behind the girth, which will cause him to move to the front and to the side at the same time. The horse's front and hind legs both cross over, in scissorlike fashion, with the front end leading slightly.

Since our only other half-pass came in Third Level Test 2 (p. 134), you may find it necessary to reinforce the required aids in your mind. Although many riders are tempted here to shift their weight to the right of the saddle to in effect "pull" the horse into a half-pass to the right, the correct way is to keep your seat square in the saddle (as it should be in all movements, whether you are doing lateral work or working on a straight line). For this half-pass to the right, your right leg should remain where it normally rests on the girth. Your inside or left leg must be positioned behind the girth to drive the haunches over. Lead (bend) the horse's head slightly using a direct rein, just enough so you can see the bulge of the horse's eye. Don't let the head tilt (indicating resistance on the horse's part) or the neck bend (indicating too much hand and not enough leg on the rider's part), or you will lose points.

Other common ways to lose points here occur when: the horse is heavy in front, so he drags behind, not showing the light, rhythmical steps he should make when he crosses over; as the rider applies the aids, the horse brings his head up above the bit; or the horse's legs do not cross over sufficiently due to lack of engagement.

[5]

KXM Medium trot
M   Collected trot

Collect the horse on the short side as you ride out of the previous half-pass, and prepare him with half-halts to cross the diagonal at the medium trot. Although the horse is being judged mainly here on his length of stride and on the quality of his gait from K to M, accuracy also plays a part in the scoring process. Sometimes riders at these higher levels concentrate so much on the specific movements and on getting the most from the horse that they lose sight of the fact that accuracy still counts. Remember that the judge expects you to ride a straight line across the diagonal here and to show him two clear transitions at K and at M. Make your medium trot as smooth as possible, showing the same length of stride in every step across the diagonal.

[6]

H–E Shoulder-in left

[7]

E Circle left 8 meters

[8]

E–D Half-pass left
A   Track left

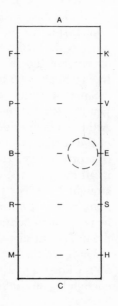

These three movements mirror the sequence we rode earlier in movements #2–#4 of this test. If you had any problems with accuracy, impulsion, or angle the first time you rode these figures, make a concerted effort to correct those problems here. Nearly every horse has a "good side" and a "bad side," so one of these sequences is bound to ride better for you than the other. If the judge sees two sloppy sequences marred by the same mistakes, he or she is going to be less than impressed with the rider's performance — as you will be when you see the scores and comments on your test sheet.

[9]

FXH Extended trot
H   Collected trot

Earlier in this test you rode a medium-to-collected trot transition across the diagonal, so the judge has something to compare your extended trot with here. To score above a 5 (sufficient) in this movement, you must show the judge more length of stride than you had in the medium trot. Your length of stride should be even more obvious here (see photo), because the extended trot is punctuated on each end with a collected trot. The difference between extension and collection is even more marked than it is between a medium and collected gait, so show the judge some drama here. The horse's head and neck should reach slightly further out and down here than they did in the medium trot, so that he can reach his ultimate length of stride by truly extending throughout his entire body, not just by reaching with his front legs.

Crossing the diagonal from F to H in the extended trot.

[10]

C Halt. Rein back 4 steps,
     proceed collected walk

Drive the horse down to a halt at C, right in front of the judge. The horse must halt square, balanced, and on the bit, with all four legs on a corner. This test doesn't specify how long you must hold the halt, so take a moment to establish it and to let the horse relax before you ask for the four steps backward. In the rein-back, the judge wants to see the horse lift each leg confidently — without hesitating or rushing — as he backs obediently by diagonals. Keep the horse parallel to the short side and straight on the track as he backs; don't allow him to drift to the inside, as judges often see. The horse must remain steadily on the bit, neither above the bit nor overflexed behind it: either of these evasions will cost you points. Remember to drive the horse forward into the collected walk while he is still in the diagonal of the fourth backward step. Do not allow him to square up first.

[11]

MRXVK Extended walk

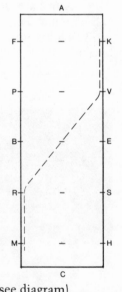

Try to show as much transition as you can as you begin this movement, because you are very close to the judge here. A true extended walk is very difficult to achieve, so you have to practice it at home. Many riders neglect to do so, because they become preoccupied with schooling the "fancier" Fourth Level movements (such as the half-pass and flying changes). You've heard this before and you will hear it again, but the walk really is the most important gait. The judge has a long stretch in which to devote his attention to your horse's length and quality of stride in the extended walk here, as you ride from M to R on the long side, cross the "short diagonal" from R to V, and continue up the other long side to the next letter at K (see diagram).

Remember to maintain contact with the horse's mouth — this is an extended walk, not a "free walk" on a loose rein. It takes a certain knack to get the horse to extend his walk without jigging or breaking into a trot (for which you will be punished severely in points lost). You can drive with your seat or urge the horse on with alternating leg pressure. This is really a case in which you have to know your horse to get the most points from the movement.

[12]

K–A Medium walk
A   Collected walk
F   Turn left

There is not much distance from K to A in which to show your horse's medium walk, so be sure to establish that gait right away, with a clear transition from the extended walk to the medium walk at K. In the medium walk the horse's strides should be somewhat shorter and higher than in the extended walk, but don't overdo it because you have to show yet another transition to the collected walk at A. If you think about this ahead of time as a walk sequence of extended-to-medium-to-collected, you will probably ride both movements #11 and #12 more smoothly.

Your final transition to the collected walk at A had better be an obvious one, because you are presented sideways to the judge, who has a clear view of you from directly across the arena at C. Proceed in the collected walk to F, where you make a smooth turn off the rail to the midpoint of that end of the arena, between F and K.

[13]

Between D & K Half-pirouette left,
**   proceed at collected walk**

[14]

Between D & F Half-pirouette right,
**   proceed at collected walk**

These two half-pirouettes are ridden at any point between the side and the center of the arena on the far end, near A. "Think" shoulder-in as you approach your first pirouette, which in this case will be to the left. Keep the horse's head leading to the inside with your inside rein, but remember that the important rein here is your outside one. It works toward the inside haunch, to lift the front end around in the walk tempo. It is especially important to keep the horse's inside hind leg in the walk tempo by driving with your inside leg on the girth. Use your outside leg behind the girth to keep the haunch in place and to prevent the horse from stepping sideways (in this case to the right) during the turn.

[15]

The collected walk

Movement #15 is not really a "movement" per se, but it counts as one in scoring. Although the quality of your horse's collected walk throughout the two previous half-pirouettes accounted for part of your score on those movements, in this movement the collected walk is the sole basis for judging. Again, this emphasizes the importance of the walk gait. So in essence you are receiving a separate score here for the manner in which your horse was tracking in movements #13 and #14. (And by the way, if a caller is reading this test for you at a competition, he or she should not announce "the collected walk" but should read directly from movement #14 to movement #16.)

[16]

D Collected canter, right lead

After your second pirouette, you are in the collected walk until you reach D (an imaginary point on the center line, between F and K), where you take the collected canter and proceed across the arena toward K on the long side. This presents a profile view to the judge, so make sure the horse is engaged and balanced, cantering in the proper controlled tempo, with his forehead approaching the vertical.

Notice that now, for the first time, the test specifies which canter lead the horse must take. Here you had better be very clear in your aids, dropping your right seatbone, driving with your right leg at the girth and positioning your left leg slightly behind the girth, so that the horse knows which lead you want. Since there is no rail here to help indicate to him which lead is "correct," and since a horse at this level must be able to take either lead in order to perform the flying changes that come later in this test, the rider must use the proper aids to "tell" the horse which lead he wants him to take. The judge will penalize you severely if your horse takes the left lead here, for you will not have executed the movement specified by the test.

[17]

K   **Track right**
K–H **Medium canter**
H   **Collected canter**

When you arrive at K in the collected canter, you turn to the right and return to the track. Immediately the horse must move into the medium canter down the long side — which isn't as easy as it seems, because you have to overcome the horse's tendency to lose impulsion as you make the turn at K — and maintain that gait all the way to H. At H the horse must collect his canter and show an obvious transition between the two gaits. It is important to collect the canter well at H to prepare for the next movement.

[18]

C   **Turn on center line**
G–E **Half-pass right**

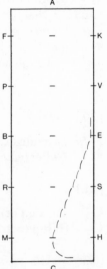

At C, right in front of the judge, you make a smooth turn in the collected canter onto the center line. At G, which is only six meters from the end of the arena and the judge's booth, you must ride a half-pass to the right (see diagram). Only one other test (Third Level Test 2, p. 139) has required the half-pass to be ridden in the canter, so this is a movement you should practice considerably at home to achieve smoothness and the proper angle. Some horses (and riders) actually prefer riding the half-pass in the canter rather than the trot, because they find it easier to maintain the impulsion.

You can prepare for this half-pass in the test by riding a little "fore-shoulder," as it is sometimes called, or as I like to describe it, "thinking shoulder-in" before you start. You want to "pre-engage" the horse on the turn, to set him up for the coming half-pass. Encourage him to engage his hindquarters and to carry his head slightly to the right, so that when he begins the lateral movement at G, he will be leading slightly with his head and shoulders. This will help him to maintain the correct angle for the half-pass, with his legs crossing over rhythmically in front and back.

Maintain the same angle from G to E, where you straighten the horse on the long side and maintain the counter-canter.

[19]

V Flying change of lead

At V, which is 12 meters down the long side from E, the horse must make a flowing (and flying) change from the counter-canter to the true canter. This is the first time the tests call for a flying change on a straight line and all of the flying changes in this test are coefficient movements. So a poor mark on this flying change — or any of the ones that follow — can adversely affect your overall test score.

For a high score in the flying change, the horse must be straight when he executes it. The change must be what judges call "true," which means that it should be made from behind, followed a split-second later by a change in front. If a horse changes in front and then a second or two later changes behind, the change is called "late." The horse's head should remain on the bit during the change and he should not wring or swish his tail (which, nonetheless, is a common resistance, even in some of the top horses in competition).

[20]

F–M Extended canter
M Collected canter

[21]

C Turn on center line
G–B Half-pass left

[22]

P Flying change of lead

You should have ridden the two corners and the short side after the flying change at V to prepare the horse in collection for the extended canter down the long side from F to M. At M you collect and ride the same half-pass-to-flying-change sequence as in movements #18 and #19 of this test.

[23]

A–C Serpentine of three loops, no change of lead

The serpentine with the counter-canter was introduced in Third Level Test 1, so you may want to refer to my previous directives for the movement there (p. 132). In this test your counter-canter is done in the second or middle loop of the serpentine, where you must keep your outside leg strong to keep the horse from making a flying change.

[24]

MXK Change rein, three changes of lead every fourth stride

This is the first time the tests have called for a series of flying changes. The test does not specify where to execute your first flying change here, so it is up to the rider. However, to ensure that you have enough strides left to get all the changes and intermediary striding in, you may need to ride the first change soon after you start across the diagonal. It is most impressive if you can space the changes so that your first and last ones are the same distance away from each side of the arena.

What is required is that the horse make three changes of lead, always on the fourth stride. The judge counts to himself as you ride, "1-2-3-4, 2-2-3-4, 3-2-3-4." If he does not see a change occur on the first number of each sequence, you lose points. If you maintain the prescribed pattern of striding and changes, you finish on the true canter lead as you reach the long side of the arena.

When this movement (which carries a coefficient) is done flowingly, it is indeed a beautiful one which represents the upper ranges of dressage. It always draws extra attention from the crowd — and from the judge, who will be counting your strides and changes to make sure they are all there. He or she will also judge you on the quality of the flying changes, marking you down if the horse rushes, anticipates, or falters in his changes of lead.

[25]

A Down center line
X Halt; rein back 4 steps,
  proceed collected canter, left lead

[26]

G Halt. Salute.

This is a variation on our normal theme of "down center line, halt, salute," this time with a four-stride rein-back at X. It is not the easiest movement in the world to ride, particularly because of its placement at the end of this long and demanding test. Your horse is no fool, and no doubt when he halts at X, his tendency will be to think that the test is over and he is done. It takes a thinking and skilled rider to keep the horse alert and responsive here.

This is also the first time the tests have called for the horse to canter forward from the rein-back, instead of proceeding in the collected walk or trot. Moreover, this test requires that the horse take the left lead here, so make your aids distinct. Ride him in collection but send him forward toward the judge, driving down to a square halt at G, where you salute.

AHSA FOURTH LEVEL TEST 2

Fourth Level Test 2 really serves to separate "the men from the boys" in dressage. It bridges the gap between the AHSA and FEI dressage tests, and includes a number of similarities to the FEI Prix St. Georges test.

[1]

A Enter collected canter
X Halt. Salute. Proceed collected trot
C Track left

This entry, which began at Third Level Test 3, remains the same throughout the international tests (including FEI Grand Prix). The horse must be in a collected canter as soon as you enter the arena (preferably before). Since you may enter on either lead, start with an advantage by showing your horse's "good side."

[2]

HXF Extended trot
F   Collected trot

You should have prepared the horse with half-halts on the short side and ridden the corner before H so that he will be straight when you start across the diagonal. At this level, the judge expects your extension to go precisely from letter to letter. The extended strides should be even and regular all the way from H to F, where you collect the trot.

[3]

KXH Counter change of hand in half-pass

[4]

MXF Counter change of hand in half-pass

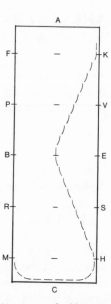

These two coefficient movements, which mirror each other, are beautiful when they are performed by a relaxed and supple horse. Use half-halts in the corner after F and along the short side to lighten and balance the horse. As you come away from the corner toward K, think shoulder-in so that the horse's head will be leading slightly (see photo). Apply your outside leg to initiate the half-pass, and steady your aids so that the horse maintains the same angle from K to X.

Just before X, straighten the horse for one stride, change the bend to the left, and starting at X, guide him into a half-pass in the opposite direction. Be sure to keep the horse's head leading in the direction of the movement and half-pass all the way to H. The difficult part is getting the horse to come clear to the track, maintaining his bend and balance without stiffening or popping a shoulder.

In this counter change of hand, the horse does a half-pass in one direction, straightens briefly at X, and continues the half-pass in the opposite direction.

[5]

V   Medium trot and circle right 20 meters
V   Collected trot
E   Turn right

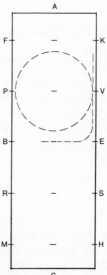

[6]

B   Track left
R   Medium trot and circle left 20 meters
R   Collected trot

This is the first time the tests call for the medium trot to be performed on a large circle, which is also required in some of the international tests, including the FEI Three-Day Event Test (p. 187).

To ride this movement correctly, the horse must be engaged and light before you come to V, where you ride off the track to begin your 20-meter circle (see diagram). Right away, from your first step on the circle, the judge expects the horse to be in a balanced and rhythmical medium trot. Pay attention to the figure, riding a full 20-meter circle that bisects the V–P line.

Begin to collect the horse a stride or two before you complete the circle at V, so that he will be ready to come back into a collected trot. Ride on to E, beginning your turn just before the letter so that you come straight onto the E–B line. From there, you ride across the arena and perform the same 20-meter medium trot circle at R.

[7]

HXF   Extended trot
F   Collected trot

This movement rides the same as in movement #2 of this test and in the Third Level tests (see directives, p. 127). This time it is even more critical to securely collect the trot at F, because the next downward transition is only a few strides away in the next movement.

[8]

A Halt. Rein back four steps, proceed collected walk

Unless the horse is really light in your hands and engaged, it will be almost impossible to achieve a balanced and smooth halt here. at A. When you get the halt, hold it a moment to let the horse relax (mentally and physically) before you ask him to back four steps. He has performed the four-step rein-back in earlier tests, but here it is more difficult because you are dealing with the momentum built up in the extended trot.

[9]

K–S Extended walk
S–C Medium walk
C   Collected walk

This is similar to the sequence of walks in Third Level Test 2 (movement #7, p. 136), but this time you ride around the edges of the arena without crossing the short diagonal. Prepare the horse for his first transition here to the extended walk at K, allowing his head and neck to reach out somewhat as you drive with your seat and back, asking for as much overstep as possible. At S, collect the horse slightly, bringing the head a little higher and showing more engagement but still maintaining some overstep. At C, the horse must become fully collected, with his forehead nearly vertical and with no overstep to his stride.

[10]

M   Turn right
Between G & H Half-pirouette right

[11]

Between G & M Half-pirouette left

These pirouettes are ridden with the same aids as described in all three Third Level tests, but here they are performed in a different location in the arena than they were in Third Level Test 1 or Test 2. In those tests, the half-pirouettes are ridden between two letters on the long side — typically H and S or M and R. In Third Level Test 3 and in this test, the movement is performed between the letter on the long side (H or M) and the letter G, which is on the center line near the judge.

Start this movement by "thinking" shoulder-in and prepare the horse to turn to the right while you lighten him with half-halts. Your important aids are the outside rein and inside leg, which keeps the forward impulsion. Your outside leg should be "on call" in case the horse starts to shift sideways.

[12]

The collected walk

This is not so much a movement as it is a scoring mechanism within the test, designed to emphasize the importance of a correct four-beat walk. When this test is called for a rider, this movement is not to be read aloud. It is there for the judge's convenience.

[13]

G Collected canter, left lead

[14]

H–K Medium canter
K   Collected canter

As you come across the center line, you must ride a transition from the collected walk to the collected canter. Make it balanced, relaxed, round, and engaged. As you turn at H to the long side, immediately show a transition into the medium canter. Ask for a lot here, but also ask for a lot of collection when you reach K, or you may overshoot the turn for the next movement.

[15]

A   Down center line
L–S Half-pass left
H   Flying change of lead

Here you ride down the center line and prepare for a half-pass left at L, which is on the center line halfway between P and V. As you approach

L, again "think" shoulder-in to lead into the half-pass at L. Keep the angle all the way to S, where you straighten the horse on the long side. Follow straight along the track to H, where the test calls for a flying change of lead. This flying change is somewhat more difficult than the changes at Third Level, because now you are riding the change on a straight line instead of coming off a circle. Since you do not have the benefit of the change of bend from the circle, your aids must be crystal clear here.

[16]

M	Proceed toward X
Between M & X	Half-pirouette right
M	Flying change of lead

Although we have performed the pirouette in the walk in earlier tests, this is the first time a test has called for the movement at canter. The horse must be light and engaged enough to canter around his hind legs (see photos). As in the pirouette in the walk, you must guide the horse around with the inside rein to keep his head leading. Use the outside rein to "tie" the neck and shoulder together and to help the horse pivot around his hind end. The horse must maintain the canter tempo, and should make three or four canter strides as he does the pirouette.

Your score for this movement will be a reflection of how tight and how rhythmical you keep the pirouette. Common faults, for which you will lose points, include: scrambling around, because the hind legs don't remain in place and describe too big a circle; not maintaining the canter all the way through the movement and trotting a few steps behind; or coming above the bit in resistance.

As you complete the pirouette and come back to the track (see diagram), straighten the horse so he is parallel to M and ask for a flying change of lead. This is the second flying change in this test, to be followed by nine more (twice as many as in Fourth Level Test 1).

The sequence of steps in the half-pirouette right, done here at the canter.

[17]

H–K Extended canter
K   Collected canter

[18]

FXH Change rein at X, flying change of lead

Ride the extended-to-collected-canter transition as in previous tests. Come around to F, where you cross the diagonal in the collected canter. A stride or two before X, alert the horse with half-halts that you are going to ask for a change. At X, reverse your canter aids smoothly so that the horse flows into a flying change. He should neither hesitate before the change nor dive into it, common faults that judges score down.

[19]

M–F Medium canter
F   Collected canter

Emphasize both transitions here, being careful to collect the horse sufficiently at F so that you will be able to make the next turn onto the center line.

[20]

A   Down center line
L–R Half-pass right
M   Flying change of lead

[21]

H   Proceed toward X
Between H & X Half-pirouette left
H   Flying change of lead

[22]

M–F Extended canter
F Collected canter

These three movements repeat those in movements #15–#17 of this test.

[23]

KXM On diagonal, three changes of lead every fourth stride

[24]

HXF On diagonal, three changes of lead every third stride

Changing from one lead to the other across the diagonal. The photo has caught the horse at the moment of change.

Collect the horse as you cross the short side, and travel straight across the diagonal so the changes will be straight (see photo). All the requirements previously discussed for a single flying change apply here, but now you must ride them in succession. In movement #23, the judge will count to himself, "1-2-3-4 . . . 2-2-3-4 . . . 3-2-3-4," expecting the horse to execute a flying change on each count of four. After the four-time changes, you again cross the diagonal and perform a series of three-time changes.

You will be scored down severely if you ride the movement inaccurately, either missing a change or changing on the wrong stride (usually late). If you apply too much outside leg during the change, the horse's hind end may jump to the side, causing you to lose points for a lack of straightness. So you see, riding the movement and making the changes is not enough for a good score here. It takes a measure of finesse as well.

[25]

A Down center line
X Halt. Rein back four steps,
  proceed at collected canter, right lead

[26]

G Halt. Salute.

This is the same final sequence as in Fourth Level Test 1. You ride in the collected canter down the center line, halt at X and ask the horse to back four steps. (The same directives for our previous rein-backs in earlier tests apply here, but in this case you are facing the judge on the center line.)

Proceed in the collected canter to G, where you halt, salute, and congratulate yourself — you are now on the threshold of international dressage.

6. Dressage for Event Riders

For combined training enthusiasts, dressage comes as the first of three tests. Since the other two tests involve jumping, there was at one time a prevailing attitude that an eventer "just had to get through dressage" to get on with the "real" competition over fences. However, several years ago it became evident that an increasing number of events were being won in the dressage arena. The emphasis in event training changed accordingly, and today the eventing community accords due respect to the dressage phase.

Some of the most successful American event riders, such as Karen Stives, were former high-level dressage competitors. A substantial number of eventers at all levels, in hopes of gaining an edge over the competition, make it a point to compete regularly at dressage shows as well. Most find that the discipline and systematic training of dressage help improve a horse's balance, attitude, and striding, both on the flat and over fences.

It can be quite a task, however, to guide a fit and enthusiastic event horse through a controlled, obedient dressage test. An experienced event horse may be difficult to keep in hand for dressage, when he would rather be out galloping cross-country fences. Still, he must do his job. The judge expects the horse to ride a true dressage test, not some imagined form of "event dressage" on a lower scale.

Remember, dressage is dressage, period. Because it is scored against a standard, the judge has to score you on what he or she sees ridden in the arena. The judge cannot make allowances for a horse's temperament, conformation, or other such factors that affect his performance.

Here is where the rider's job comes in: to know his horse and to prepare for the test, especially in warm-up, in a manner compatible with the horse's temperament. A high-strung event horse who is extremely fit may take several hours of work on the show grounds to "unwind" before he can perform a relaxed dressage test. Such was the case with the USET event horse Bally Cor in the 1976 Olympics. The mare performed the best dressage test of her career there and won the individual gold under rider Tad Coffin, who had spent the better part of the day riding Bally to settle her.

USET Three-Day captain J. Michael Plumb (mounted) shares a relaxed moment in the warm-up area with USCTA president Denny Emerson. A veteran like Plumb knows exactly how much to work each horse before a dressage test, which is the key to obtaining the best performance.

Had the rider not taken that initiative, Olympic history might have been written differently. Granted, you may not be in training for the Olympics, but there is nothing wrong with preparing for a dressage test as though you were. It all has to start somewhere.

At the national levels of eventing, the United States Combined Training Association uses the following AHSA dressage tests:

Novice division— AHSA 1983 Training Level Test 1 or
AHSA Training Level Test 2
Training division— AHSA 1983 Training Level Test 3 or
AHSA 1983 First Level Test 1
Preliminary division— AHSA 1983 First Level Test 2 or
AHSA 1983 First Level Test 3

Competitors in the upper divisions of eventing — Intermediate and Advanced — ride special dressage tests designed for the experienced event horse. The Intermediate division uses the AHSA 1976 Three-Day Dressage Test, which incorporates a number of movements from the Second and Third Level tests. The Advanced division rides the FEI 1975 Three-Day Event Dressage Test (p. 186), which incorporates 20 movements of medium difficulty, most of them found in the latter stages of Third Level.

AHSA 1976 THREE-DAY EVENT DRESSAGE TEST (INTERMEDIATE LEVEL)

[1]

A Enter at working canter
X Halt — immobility — salute.
   Proceed at working trot.

You may enter with the horse on either lead, but he must be balanced and straight as soon as he starts down the center line at A. Almost invariably in this test, horses enter bent in the direction of the lead, which means an automatic loss of points. Since the judge is sitting straight ahead of you on the C–A line, he can easily see whether the horse is straight.

The judge is also looking for a balanced working canter, which will affect the way the horse moves into the second part of this movement — the halt. An unbalanced horse will have difficulty going directly from canter to halt and is likely to insert a few trot steps before arriving at the halt (which will probably not be square).

So you can see here the interrelation of dressage movements: one thing really does lead to another. An unbalanced entry can drastically affect the quality of the movements that follow. And as far as the judge is concerned, the rider who enters the arena on an unbalanced horse has not done an adequate job of preparation. It behooves you, therefore, not to start your test on the wrong foot.

Again make sure the horse is balanced and straight as you make the transition from the halt up to the working trot. Keep the horse between your legs so that he stays on the center line, rather than allowing him to wobble to one side or the other during the transition or as he proceeds down the center line toward the judge.

[2]

C Track to the left
A Down center line
X Circle to the right 10 meters diameter,
followed immediately by circle left
10 meters diameter

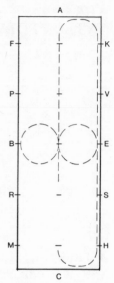

At C you turn left, riding deep into your next corner so that the horse is straight as he trots all the way up the long side (see diagram). You have two more turns (which are ridden on the arc of a 10-meter circle), first in the corner after K and again at A, where you turn down the center line. All this bending in the corners should have helped supple and prepare the horse for the major part of this movement: the figure eight in the center of the arena.

As you approach X, use half-halts to alert the horse that a change is coming and to lighten him in front. You must really "ride" the horse as he turns onto that first circle, for his tendency may be to slow his tempo or shorten his stride. Another common fault here is for the horse to bend outward at the neck and "pop a shoulder" to the outside of the circle, a resistance that will cost you points. To avoid this, keep a firm outside rein and maintain the bend through the horse's body with your legs and inside rein.

In order to make this a full 10-meter circle, you must ride all the way out to the edge of the arena (see diagram). Many competitors have a tendency here to ride an egg-shaped circle instead of a round one, which brings them back on the center line too soon. Ridden correctly, the first circle brings you back at X for one horse's length. Use this brief interval to change the bend, and then ride the same circle to the left.

You may recall that we rode this same figure eight in movement #3 of AHSA Second Level Test 2 (p. 100), but that it was worded somewhat differently in the test, which reads:

X Circle right 10 meters
X Circle left 10 meters

The difference in wording means nothing more than "six of one, half a dozen of the other," but it is worth noting so that you do not become confused later in this test when the semantics change even more. The event tests are worded and organized somewhat differently than the "straight" dressage tests, but by and large they include the same movements.

The figure eight, of course, is ridden the same way no matter how it is described. In this test it is executed in the working trot (as opposed to the collected trot in Second Level), so you may find it slightly more difficult to ride a perfectly round circle because the horse will be covering the same distance in fewer strides, which means less room for correction between one stride and the next.

[3]

C   **Track to the right**
M–B **Shoulder-in**
B   **Circle to the right 20 meters diameter at medium trot**

There is a lot to be judged in this movement, which incorporates two rather difficult exercises: the shoulder-in and the medium trot on the circle. Both have been discussed in earlier tests — the shoulder-in was introduced in AHSA First Level Test 4 (p. 81) and the 20-meter medium trot circle in Fourth Level Test 2 (p. 165) — but in those tests the two exercises are scored as separate movements. The dressage tests for event riders have a tendency to combine two or more such exercises into one movement. Unless your riding is precise and consistent here, it may be difficult for the judge to arrive at a score that accurately reflects the horse's performance throughout the entire endeavor. In other words, you're really going to have to work for this mark.

Since you are moving away from the judge in this shoulder-in, he or she will be looking to see if the horse is moving on three distinct tracks. The judge also wants to see the proper poll-to-tail bend all the way from M to B, which unfortunately we judges do not see as often as we would like. A common fault here is for the horse to be bent only in the neck and not in the body, which will lower your score and will cause problems when you try to move into the 20-meter circle at B.

A smart rider will take advantage of the shoulder-in, riding the movement correctly in order to lighten, engage, and collect the horse so he will be able to stretch into a medium trot immediately when you begin the circle at B. Since the shoulder-in has presumably already established the bend through the horse's body, it should be fairly simple to guide him onto the circle. But you may have to work for the medium trot, by driving with your back and seat so that you get sufficient lengthening. Try to keep your aids consistent here, so that the horse maintains the same rhythm all the way around the 20-meter circle.

[4]

P   **Working trot**
A   **Down center line**
D–B   **Half-pass to the right**

Your medium trot continues a few strides after you finish the circle and return to the track. At the next letter (P), the test calls for the working trot, so the judge expects to see a transition here. Show him one by getting the horse back in hand, but don't lose the impulsion as you continue down the long side and make your turns onto the center line.

The "meat" of this movement comes next, in the half-pass. It is the same movement as is ridden in AHSA Third Level Test 2 (p. 134) and in both of the Fourth Level tests, but here it is ridden in the working trot instead of in collection. In this test the half-pass begins at D, which is a point on the center line only six meters in from the end of the arena at A (see diagram of large arena). Therefore, you have only that short distance to prepare the horse with half-halts for this demanding lateral movement.

Establish the half-pass right away at D, using the aids discussed in the Third and Fourth Level tests, and drive the horse across the arena to B. Many riders have trouble here with the horse "dragging." When the hind end isn't light enough, it does not cross over sufficiently for the half-pass. As a result, the front end precedes the hind end too much. To avoid this, keep your outside leg behind the girth to push the haunches over.

Another factor in judging this movement is the requirement that the horse's head must lead slightly. What makes this half-pass difficult is that the horse must lead with his head to the right; it would be so much easier to cross the arena in a leg-yield position with the horse's head bent away from the direction of travel! But, again, no one ever said dressage was easy.

The judge has a number of other things to consider in evaluating your half-pass: Did the horse's body remain almost parallel to the sides of the arena? Did his legs cross over, both front and hind? Did he maintain a consistent rhythm and tempo? Did he move in balance? Was he truly on the bit, without resistance? This is a lot to look for in the relatively short distance from D to B, so you should make the most of your time because points can be gained or lost very quickly here.

[5]

B–C Working trot
C   Halt — rein back 4 steps — proceed at working trot without halting

Here you take the rail in the working trot and follow it around to where the judge is sitting at C. If you had problems with engagement and forwardness earlier in the test, it should come more easily here, thanks to the side-effects of the half-pass.

When you arrive at C, the test calls for the same halt and four-step rein-back ridden in several tests, beginning with AHSA Second Level Test 4 (movement #10, p. 117). This is a chance to make some points if you will just think ahead. Begin with half-halts several strides away from C to lighten the horse in front. Drive the horse with your seat into a balanced halt, so that he is square not only in front but also behind.

Many riders make the mistake here of halting too soon. The judge expects you to halt with your body (not the horse's nose) at C, which demonstrates accuracy. At this stage of training the horse is certainly capable of coming to a halt when asked, so there is no reason — except sloppy riding — for an imprecise halt here.

Hold the halt a moment to let the horse relax, and then ask him for four diagonal steps backward. For maximum points, the horse should show a long stride as he lifts each leg confidently backward, while remaining on the bit and in balance. The judge, who is right beside you at C, will watch to see if the horse remains straight on the track as he backs. If he steps toward the inside of the arena, as many horses have a tendency to do here, you will lose points.

Remember that in the diagonal of the fourth step, the horse should move forward into the working trot without squaring up. If you practice this at home, you stand to make a significant gain in points here, because the majority of riders do it poorly. This is a precision exercise that any properly schooled horse can score well in. The rider should take advantage of this, especially if his horse is not a fancy mover who can make up points elsewhere in the test.

[6]

H–E Shoulder-in
E   Circle to the left 20 meters diameter at medium trot

[7]

V   Working trot
A   Down center line
D–E Half-pass to the left

This sequence mirrors that in movements #3 and #4 of this test. My previous directives apply.

[8]

ECM Working trot
MXK Lengthen stride in trot (rising)
K   Working trot

[9]

KAF Working trot
FXH Lengthen stride in the trot
HC   Working trot

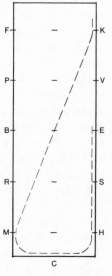

Here we have a series of transitions from the working to the lengthened trot. Your first lengthening from M to K is done rising; the second one is done sitting. In both movements #8 and #9, you should use half-halts as you go around the short side to balance the horse and to lighten him in front. Otherwise, if he is heavy on the forehand, your "lengthening" is likely to be a running trot, with a tempo that is too fast and a stride of insufficient length.

On the first lengthening, don't forget to begin rising right at the letter M, as you start across the diagonal. Many riders like to begin this lengthening with a few steps sitting and then begin to rise, because having their seat in the saddle helps them drive the horse into a longer gait. Technically this is wrong, since the test calls for you to begin rising immediately at M, but you can probably get away with it if you

A trot lengthening across the diagonal, with the horse in the proper frame and attitude.

don't prolong the sitting more than a stride or two. Be forewarned, though, that some judges may notice and mark you down accordingly.

When you reach K, resume the sitting trot and bring the horse back to a working gait. Be sure to show the judge some semblance of a transition here, even if the horse did not produce a dramatic lengthening. When you reach F, you have another chance at the lengthening, this time at sitting trot. Make the most of this opportunity to use your back, seat, and legs to drive the horse forward, taking care not to override him into a canter. When you reach the long side at H, show a transition back to the working trot and continue around the arena to C, where the judge is sitting.

[10]

C	Medium walk
MXK	Extended walk
KA	Medium walk

This is a series of transitions in the walk, from medium to extended and back to medium. The first transition occurs at C, right in front of the judge. It is not an easy one by any means, because you are coming from the working trot and very likely have lots of impulsion due to the lengthenings in the previous two movements. When you alert the horse with half-halts for the transition to a medium walk at C, he will probably be expecting a halt or at most a working walk. So as you drive him down to a walk, you must keep enough forward impulsion with your seat and legs to attain a considerable overstep in the medium walk. Otherwise, you will lose points rapidly here.

Sometimes other problems arise here when the horse has become tense or excited from the lengthened work. He may jig a little or even pace a few steps during the transition at C, which constitutes a resistance and must be marked down.

You have a chance to atone somewhat for a poor transition at C as you cross the diagonal in the extended walk from M to K. It takes a skillful rider and a well-trained horse to maintain regularity in the extended walk all the way across the diagonal. The horse should lengthen his frame, reaching slightly down and out with his head and neck, as he oversteps to his maximum. To score well here you must establish the extended walk right away, because the judge is situated in a position that allows him to determine the horse's overstep only from M to X. After that, he has a limited vantage point and will not be able to reward you for improving the extended walk on the second half of the diagonal.

At K comes another transition back to the medium walk. This can be tricky to ride, because you have to show a transition to a shorter gait, yet it must still be longer than a working gait. The judge expects your medium walk to be more engaged, with the horse's topline slightly higher than it was in the extended walk. This calls for precision riding.

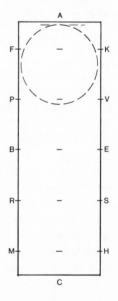

[11]

A Working canter. Circle to the left 20 meters

This basic dressage movement, which comes in the very first test at Training Level Test 1, may come as a bit of a breather to you at this point in the test. In the lower-level tests, however, the canter circle is taken from a working trot, instead of the medium walk that precedes it in this test.

The judge expects your horse to move into the canter smoothly and with no trot steps here. Since he has a profile view of you, make sure you execute the canter transition right at the letter A. Accuracy counts in the scoring, so you will lose points if your horse takes the canter late (or early, which is not usually the case).

As you ride along the short side in the working canter, remember not to ride into the corner this time. It is so ingrained in some competitors to ride into the corners that it becomes almost automatic, and a number of riders seem to forget here that a circle doesn't have corners. Make this a full 20-meter circle by just coming tangent to the circle at four points and by riding two meters beyond the V–P line (see diagram). Judges often witness an egg-shaped circle here, which is the result of riding into the corners and then turning too soon.

I find it interesting (and disconcerting) to note that so many Inter-mediate-level eventers can execute the more demanding Fourth Level movements in this test relatively well, yet for some reason they throw away precious points with sloppy riding on a basic 20-meter canter circle. Just because this is a simpler movement does not make it any less important to the judge, so it stands to reason that you should put in the necessary effort to gain a decent mark here.

[12]

A–C Serpentine 3 loops; the first and third true canter, the second counter-canter

This is basically the same canter serpentine as in Fourth Level Test 1 (p. 161), except in this case you begin on the left lead. Do not ride into the corner but maintain a continual loop, keeping your outside leg on the horse's side to discourage him from changing leads. Many horses have a tendency, especially in the second (middle) loop, to change leads in front.

The judge will also be evaluating the shape of your serpentine. Try to make three equal loops, with the B–E line bisecting the middle loop. This is a good place for the rider to make his own quick evaluation of his serpentine, and to make any adjustments in distance before he rides into the third and final loop. If you wait too long, there won't be enough time to compensate and you will end up with the last loop being either too small or too large. Actually, a three-loop serpentine is three 20-meter half-circles.

As you ride into the final loop, remember to not ride into the corner but to maintain the continuous curve of the serpentine, which finishes in front of the judge at C.

[13]

C–H Working canter
HXF Lengthen stride
F   Working trot

Ride past C in the canter, and this time do ride into the corner as you turn onto the long side. When you reach the letter H, establish a transition to a lengthened canter as soon as possible. As in the previous trot lengthenings in this test, you want the horse to stretch his entire body out into a longer frame, covering more ground with each stride.

A stride or two before you reach the end of the diagonal, prepare the horse with half-halts for the transition to the working trot at F. Unless the horse has become heavy in his lengthening, this is not usually a difficult transition.

[14]

A Working canter — circle to the right 20 meters

The rider is asking the horse to bend onto the 20-meter circle at the canter. The bend should be less pronounced in the neck and more evenly distributed through the horse's body.

[15]

A–C Serpentine 3 loops; the first and third true canter,
the second counter-canter

[16]

C–M Working canter
MXK Lengthen stride
K   Working trot

These three movements repeat the same sequence we just rode in movements #11–#13 of this test.

[17]

A Down center line
G Halt — immobility — salute

Here your halt is at G, which means you are being exposed to the judge on the center line for a rather long time. He has plenty of time to evaluate your horse's stride, balance, and consistency, so keep both legs evenly on the horse's sides to keep him from wobbling to either side of the center line.

As you approach G, begin to prepare the horse for a halt, but be careful not to ask too soon. Many riders here have a tendency to halt several meters before G, which must be scored down as an inaccuracy. Although G is a point on the center line, it is not difficult to locate if you think about it as being six meters in from the judge at C, on the center line between H and M. Until you become more comfortable with the location of G, spot one of those letters (H or M) through the corner of your eye as you ride down the center line, and please do not halt until you get there.

1975 FEI THREE-DAY EVENT DRESSAGE TEST (ADVANCED LEVEL)

[1]

A Enter at working canter
X Halt — immobility — salute
   Proceed at working trot

You may enter the arena with the horse on either lead, but be sure he is cantering straight. Since the judge is sitting straight ahead of you at C, he will notice if the horse is bent to one side as he canters down the center line (as is often the case).

It is also important to make sure the horse goes directly from canter to halt at X. Three-day horses often perform this movement as if it read canter-trot-halt, or sometimes even canter-trot-walk-halt. The judge must penalize you unless the horse goes from canter to halt.

As in any dressage test, the horse is expected to halt square and in balance, maintaining the same frame he had in the canter. His head should remain reliably on the bit in the halt and during the transition into the working trot.

USET Three-Day captain J. Michael Plumb, considered the most experienced event rider in the world, guides his horse into a beautifully balanced trot down the center line after the halt at X.

[2]

C   Track to the left
S   Medium trot
EBE Circle to the left 20 meters diameter
E–V Medium trot

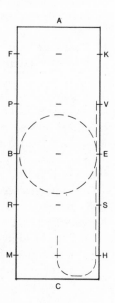

In the AHSA dressage tests, tracking to the left at C would have been part of the first movement. Here, it initiates the second movement, which leads into the medium trot. The judge wants to see a smooth yet distinct transition from working to medium trot at S.

With your medium trot already established, you continue it as you ride into a full 20-meter circle at E. The horse must be balanced and regular, not uneven behind, as often happens when you ask for a medium trot on a circle. From the circle, you maintain that gait until you reach V (see diagram).

[3]

V Working trot
A Down center line
L Circle to the left 10 meters diameter

This entire movement is ridden in the working trot sitting. Your turn at A onto the center line should be smooth and balanced, so that the horse arrives accurately on the C–A line. At L, you curve off the center line to the left for a 10-meter circle. Take care that the horse does not "pop a shoulder" here as he begins or ends the circle. He should maintain the same frame and stride throughout the 10-meter circle that he had when going straight.

[4]

L–S Half-pass left

The half-pass must begin as soon as you complete the previous circle. It is ridden as described in my directives for AHSA Third Level Test 2 (p. 134).

[5]

C Halt — rein back 5 steps — proceed at working trot without halting

Remember that the initial movement here is a trot-to-halt transition, so there should be no intermediary walk steps. The horse should halt balanced and square, with his weight distributed equally on all four legs. After you establish the halt, ask the horse to back exactly five steps. The more you can get him to lengthen his stride while backing, the better the judge will like it.

Often judges see a horse take two or three good steps backward, then begin to resist and shorten his stride, whch results in unevenness. Other horses may react to the rider's aids by coming above the bit and backing with their head in the air, or by overflexing and coming behind the bit, both of which are forms of resistance that will be penalized.

From the diagonal of the fifth step, the horse should move forward into the working trot without hesitation.

[6]

R   Medium trot
REB Circle to the right 20 meters diameter
B–P Medium trot

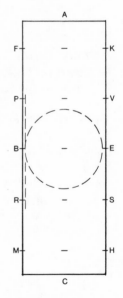

This is a demanding movement, ridden entirely in the medium trot. My directives for the 20-meter circle in the medium trot were discussed in AHSA Fourth Level Test 2 (p. 165).

[7]

P Working trot
A Down center line
L Circle to the right 10 meters diameter

[8]

L–R Half-pass right

Well-known event rider Mike Huber guides his horse into the half-pass to the right. The horse's legs are crossing over correctly and he is looking in the direction of travel, but he shows some resistance here.

[9]

C Halt — immobility 5 seconds — proceed at working trot

These three movements mirror movements #3–#5 of this test, with the exception of the halt sequence at C. Movement #9 requires the horse to remain in the halt for five seconds, instead of backing five steps as before. Many times horses here start to back automatically, because they remember the earlier sequence, and the rider compensates by pushing the horse forward. This will lose you handfuls of points, because any motion during the five seconds means that you are not maintaining the immobility of the halt as specified.

[10]

HXF Change rein at extended trot (rising)
F Working trot

[11]

KXM Change rein at extended trot
M Working trot

These two movements have the same sequence, but note that the first extended trot across the diagonal is done rising. It doesn't matter which diagonal you are on — just make sure you are on one. If the judge finds you sitting to the trot instead of rising, you will be penalized two points for an error. The same goes if you post during the second extension instead of sitting. The rider cannot "write his own test" here.

You should have prepared for each extension by using half-halts on the short side and in the corners to engage and lighten the horse. This helps make it possible for him to show an immediate extension at the first letter and maintain the gait continuously across the diagonal. If the horse is not adequately prepared for the extended trot, he is prone to make any of the following common faults in this movement: breaking into the canter, giving a little "skip" or some other irregularity, going wide behind, or not showing a sufficient extension (because he is not engaged).

No matter what happened across the diagonal, try to show a definite transition back to the working trot at the specified letter. And if your first extension had problems, try to atone for them in your second one. Usually the second extension is better than the first, because when you are sitting you can use your back and seat to drive the horse forward on every stride. The judge will therefore be expecting to see an improvement, and he is likely to be rather harsh in his scoring if he sees you make the same mistake twice in a row. That means you are a passenger, not a rider, which is inexcusable at this level.

[12]

C   **Medium walk**
HSXPF **Change rein at extended walk**
F   **Medium walk**

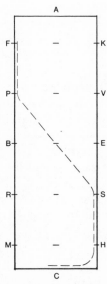

This movement can be more difficult than you might expect, especially if you are dealing with a very fit and tuned event horse. The horse is likely to be excited and full of impulsion after the two extended trots he has just performed, so he may try to argue a little when you ask him to come down to a medium walk at C. If a horse is tense going into the walk here, he will probably tighten up and shorten his gait, perhaps even doing a few pacing steps. This is not going to win you any points with the judge, since he is using this movement to evaluate your horse's gaits.

As you ride across the short diagonal, the horse must stretch his frame and stride into an extended walk. The judge wants to see as much overstep as possible (ideally, from eight to ten inches), without the horse jigging or breaking into a trot. It is up to the rider to communicate feelings of relaxation to the horse in order for this movement to be performed well.

[13]

A Working canter — circle to the right 10 meters diameter

Many event horses, especially those which compete strictly in the Advanced division, learn to anticipate this movement in the test. As they approach the letter A, they become over-anxious to take the canter, so they may "compromise" with a pacing gait or a tense walk. This again will hurt your score in several ways: the collective marks for gaits and submission, and your mark for the movement itself.

Instead, the horse should remain in the medium walk and flow smoothly into the canter at A, where he must immediately begin a 10-meter circle. Make the circle precise. Since the judge is sitting on the C–A line, he can see the quarterlines. If you override or underride the first or second quarterline, you will be penalized for inaccuracy.

[14]

**A–C Serpentine 3 loops; the first and third true canter,
the second counter-canter**

This is ridden exactly the same way as described in AHSA First Level
Test 2 (p. 59). Usually the problems come in the second loop, when the
horse is in the counter-canter. Horses that are somewhat stiff or resistant here have a tendency to throw their haunches to the outside, bent
almost in a renvers as they make the counter-canter. Sometimes they
go into a four-beat canter at this point, which will be punished severely.
As you finish the second loop, make sure it comes all the way out to B.
Horses that are tense often try to cut to the inside here, without making
the full loop. Remember, a serpentine is actually three 20-meter half-
circles.

[15]

MXK Change rein at extended canter
K   Working trot

Here the horse has to really "dig in" and extend his stride in the canter.
Oftentimes the tendency is for the horse to just speed up instead of
extending, but the judge is sure to catch this and mark you down for it.
Some judges even count how many strides you take across the diagonal,
because a horse in extension covers the same distance with fewer
strides.

When you reach the other side of the arena at K, the horse must come
down to a working trot. Considering the impulsion of the extended
canter, this may be easier said than done. When you ask for the trot,
the horse may switch leads behind instead, unless you keep him bent
to the right and engaged.

[16]

A Working canter — circle to the left 10 meters diameter

[17]

**A–C Serpentine three loops; the first and third true canter,
the second counter-canter**

[18]

HXF Change rein at extended canter
F   Working trot

This is the same sequence you rode in movements #13–#15 of this test. My same directives apply.

[19]

A Down center line
L Working canter (right)

As you ride down the center line in the working trot, you must take a right-lead canter at L. The main purpose of this movement is to ascertain that you can keep the horse straight as he makes the trot-to-canter transition. The judge is sitting straight ahead at C, so he will be sure to notice if the horse swings his haunches off the center line.

[20]

G Halt — immobility — salute
Leave arena at a walk on a long rein at A

This is similar to the halt-salute-exit sequence of many of the AHSA dressage tests outlined earlier in this book. While most of them end with a trot-to-halt transition, this test requires you to go from canter to halt, as in the AHSA Fourth Level tests.

7. Interpreting Your Scores

Ellin Dixon-Rosendale at the 1984 Olympic selection trials. Some of the movements performed by these FEI-level horses and riders are introduced at Third and Fourth Level, and show the caliber of excellence that readers should strive for. The first picture shows Dixon-Rosendale saluting the judge, then performing a flying change of lead, and third, thanking her horse for his outstanding performance after leaving the arena.

Dressage tests are scored on a point scale of zero to 10 (with 10 being the highest score possible) for each movement. The points are tallied, multiplied by a coefficient when applicable, and added to the collective marks. The total number of points earned, divided by the number of possible points, results in a percentage score for the test.

In combined training events, the dressage score is converted to a penalty-point basis, so the lower the test score, the better. In pure dressage competitions, the highest score is the winner.

Newcomers to dressage competition may find it difficult to interpret their scores, because they bear no parallel to the test-score percentages we grew accustomed to in school. While percentage scores in the 80's and 90's indicate good academic grades, they are rare indeed in the dressage world. A high "report card" for dressage would show scores in the 60's or 70's, with the majority of scores falling between 45 and 65.

Generally you can use these guidelines: If you are scoring below 50 percent, your horse is not ready for competition at that level. Go home and do some more training. Scores between 50 and 60 percent mean that the horse is performing adequately at that level, but that you still have room for improvement. You may continue to compete at that level until your scores are consistently in the 60's, at which point it is time to move up.

Another way to assess your progress is by the individual scores given each movement on your test sheet and by the judge's comments noted beside the scores. The scale of marks and their definitions are as follows:

10 Excellent
 9 Very good
 8 Good
 7 Fairly good
 6 Satisfactory
 5 Sufficient
 4 Insufficient
 3 Fairly bad
 2 Bad
 1 Very bad
 0 Not executed

Since English is a rather imprecise language, some of these adjectives are at best vague. Competitors (and some inexperienced judges) may be hard-pressed to distinguish the shades of meaning between such terms as "fairly good" and "good," or "sufficient" and "insufficient." An experienced judge, however, carries a clear mental picture of what constitutes a "6" extended trot versus a "7." Instead of trying to rank one ride against the next, the judge scores against a standard, which gives your marks meaning.

But to a degree, judging is by its nature subjective. Here is how I look at the scale of marks:

0 — "Not executed" means that you did not do what the test calls for in that particular movement. If you were supposed to show a working trot from A to F, but the horse cantered that distance instead, there is no question that the movement was not executed and your score is zero. Differences of opinion arise, however, when the test calls for a 20-meter canter circle to the right, but the horse goes around on the left lead. Some judges will score that a 1 or 2 because you did do a circle and the horse did canter, but I feel it deserves a score of zero because the right-lead circle was not executed.

1 — "Very bad" means you are getting from letter to letter, but not in the proper manner. For example, say the test calls for a canter half-pass from the center line, with a flying change when you reach the long side of the arena. When you ask for the half-pass, the horse resists by rearing, tossing his head, and backing instead of moving laterally. Eventually he makes it to the long side, where he bucks into the flying change. This, to me, is unquestionably a "1."

2 — "Bad" becomes a question of degree. I would give a score of 2 in situations like these: In a canter pirouette, the horse breaks to the trot. Or during a turn on the haunches, the horse takes one correct step and then finishes with a turn on the forehand.

3 — "Fairly bad" is better than bad, but still not acceptable. Say the test calls for four changes of lead every third stride across the diagonal. You do the four changes, but only the first and last are three-stride changes. The middle two were only two strides apart. You made two mistakes, but you did do the four flying changes prescribed. Other examples of a "3" would be when the horse breaks to the canter in the middle of an otherwise good extended trot, or when you are in an extended walk and the horse jigs into a trot.

4 — "Insufficient" means that in the judge's mind, the horse's execution of the movement was slightly lacking in quality. An often-seen example of a "4" occurs when the horse is supposed to go down the long side in the medium canter, but he shows a minimal transition at the outset and then coasts around the end. The horse is cantering, maintaining straightness, and is on the correct lead, but he is not showing enough length of stride to constitute a true medium canter. Another case of "insufficient" may occur during a horse's entry into the arena. Instead of coming to a direct halt from the trot or canter, the horse may shuffle through a walk, not halt square, or perhaps move behind. If so, his score is at best a 4.

5 — "Sufficient" means that the performance was acceptable. In the halt sequence described above, the horse would have probably scored a 5 had his halt been relatively square and immobile. A "sufficient" pirouette occurs when the horse does cross over but slows down his walk tempo. His score will lower to a 3 or 4 if he loses the walk rhythm and sticks his inside hind leg in the ground.

6 — "Satisfactory" is the first of our positive marks, but it usually means you are lacking some brilliance or fine-tuning that the judge was looking for. Here are some examples: The test calls for the horse to turn to the right at B, cross the center of the arena, and turn to the left at E. He shows an ordinary trot, but he is on the bit and executes his turns with smoothness and precision. In another test, you turn onto the center line and ride a 10-meter circle to the left at I. Your circle is slightly egg-shaped, but the horse is moving nicely under himself, keeps the rhythm, and remains on the bit throughout most of the movement.

Another example comes in a trot extension, when the horse shows a developing gait with some overstep, yet lacking full extension. If he stays in balance, rhythmical, and on the bit, I will give him a 6. Similarly in the canter depart from the short side to the long side, a 6 is likely if the horse stays on the bit and makes a smooth transition but executes it in the corner when he is not quite parallel to the side of the arena.

7 — "Fairly good" would have been the score for the same canter depart had it occurred at the letter, with the horse straight and balanced, and if the horse later bent properly into the corner. Other "7" situations are when the horse performs a rhythmical, balanced, and accurate 10-meter circle in the canter; or in the half-pass, when the horse crosses over and remains balanced and on the bit throughout most of the movement. If there is some wavering of the angle of the half-pass, his score drops to a 6.

8 — "Good" means that you have satisfied the requirements and executed the movement with some finesse. An extended trot gets an 8 when the horse shows cadence and brilliance, moving his legs in a parallelogram, going exactly from letter to letter. When judging internationally, we see so many good extended trots that 8 becomes almost a floor figure for the movement.

9 — "Very good" would have been the judgment on the previous extended trot had it shown more "hop" — that is, a higher degree of brilliance, with more extension before the front foot lands, and full engagement behind. A "9" extended canter would go precisely from letter-to-letter, with the stride increasing four or five feet in length. The horse stays straight and drives down smoothly into collection at the end of the long side.

10 — "Excellent" scores are seen occasionally, usually in international competition. Most often they occur at the start or finish of a test, when the horse comes down the center line absolutely straight, in balance and rhythm, full of impulsion, and goes directly from canter to a square halt. He stands absolutely still, like a statue, patently proud of himself. A "10," as in the movie that came out several years ago by the same name, means the ultimate in perfection. Obviously, perfection isn't something you can expect to see every day, either in life or in the dressage arena. But a "10" isn't unattainable, so there's nothing wrong with shooting for the moon.

So, there are 11 numbers that can be used for scoring dressage tests,

Robert Dover and Romantico, who competed for the USET in the Los Angeles Olympics, in the medium trot (first photo), and leaving the arena.

and I firmly believe judges should use the full range. Inexperienced judges are often overly cautious and tend to give out only middle scores — 4 if the movement wasn't good, 5 if it was okay, and 6 if it was good. This isn't fair to the riders because it is not an accurate measure of their performance, and it usually results in a number of horses tying for the same score or ribbon.

As the judge observes your ride, he or she must arrive at a single score for each numbered movement. When there are two parts to one movement, such as an eight-meter circle into a haunches-in, the judge faces a dilemma unless the rider has been very consistent. What if the circle is a 7 but the haunches-in is a 3 or 4? In that case, the judge must average it out and give you a 5 or 6.

Similarly, in the lower levels, if you ride an accurate 20-meter circle but fail to straighten the horse out on the long side afterwards, that detracts from your score for the circle movement. Remember, you are still being scored for the movement until the next one begins. Just because there is some space between figures in the lower levels doesn't mean you are on break.

In fact, the judge is likely to use the interval between movements to form some impressions for your collective marks, which appear at the bottom of your score sheet and carry a coefficient of two. The horse will be scored on his gaits, impulsion, and submission, while the rider is evaluated on his position, seat, and the effectiveness of his aids. Since these marks are the most subjective area of the test, there are no hard and fast rules here. Generally, however, the collective marks will not be far off from your average scores throughout the test.

If you refer to the sample score sheet for AHSA First Level Test 1 on p. 205, you will notice that a column for "directive ideas" appears beside the test movements. These directives reveal the main judging emphasis for each movement. Beside them is your point score, which is further explained by the judge's handwritten remarks in the far right column. A judge is not obligated to offer these remarks, but may do so as a courtesy to help the rider understand why he received a certain score and to point out areas which need improvement.

Knowing how to read and interpret your test results is important, because it makes dressage competition a learning experience rather than just a try for a ribbon. The sample score sheet in this chapter shows that the horse executed all the required movements of AHSA First Level Test 1, but did so basically without brilliance. The horse had some nice moments, particularly in the 15-meter canter circles, but the rider obviously did not push for perfection. Such a cautious ride results in a mediocre score of 50 percent, which is neither embarrassing nor gold-medal material. Yet the rider should not be discouraged, because these test results are representative of horses who have just moved up from Training to First Level.

All an average score indicates is that you have to go back and do some more homework, which is really what dressage is all about — even at the highest levels — a constant striving for perfection.

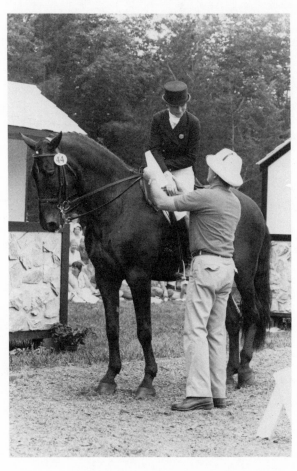

General Burton hands a USET certificate to a rider who competed in the final Olympic selection trials, in June, 1984.

Sample Score Sheet

Diagrams:

Small Arena
Large Arena

FIRST LEVEL, TEST 1

NEW MOVEMENTS:
15 M CIRCLES AT TROT AND CANTER
LENGTHEN STRIDE IN THE WALK AND TROT

NO.

		TEST	DIRECTIVE IDEAS	POINTS	CO EFFICIENT	TOTAL	REMARKS
1	A	ENTER WORKING TROT SITTING	STRAIGHTNESS ON CENTER LINE. TRANSITIONS. QUALITY OF HALT AND TURN AT C.	4			Not straight Not square Resistance
	X	HALT. SALUTE. PROCEED WORKING TROT SITTING					
	C	TRACK RIGHT					
2	B	CIRCLE RIGHT 15 M	QUALITY OF TROT. ROUNDNESS AND SIZE OF CIRCLE.	6			
3	KXM	LENGTHEN STRIDE IN TROT RISING	STRAIGHTNESS. QUALITY OF LENGTHENED TROT AND OF TRANSITIONS.	4	2		Running
	M	WORKING TROT SITTING					
4	E	CIRCLE LEFT 15 M	QUALITY OF TROT. ROUNDNESS AND SIZE OF CIRCLE.	5			Too small
5	A	HALT 5 SECONDS, PROCEED WORKING WALK	QUALITY OF HALT AND TRANSITIONS.	5			Walked to halt
6	FXH	LENGTHEN STRIDE IN WALK	STRAIGHTNESS. QUALITY OF LENGTHENED WALK AND OF TRANSITIONS.	4	2		Irregular
	H	WORKING WALK					
7	C	WORKING TROT	CALMNESS AND SMOOTHNESS OF DEPART.	5			took canter on corner
	M	WORKING CANTER RIGHT LEAD					
8	B	CIRCLE RIGHT 15 M	QUALITY OF CANTER. ROUNDNESS AND SIZE OF CIRCLE.	7			
9	KXM	CHANGE REIN	STRAIGHTNESS. CALMNESS AND SMOOTHNESS OF TRANSITIONS.	5			stiff transition at X
	X	WORKING TROT SITTING					
	M	WORKING CANTER LEFT LEAD					
10	E	CIRCLE LEFT 15 M	QUALITY OF CANTER. ROUNDNESS AND SIZE OF CIRCLE.	7			
11	FXH	CHANGE REIN ACROSS DIAGONAL	STRAIGHTNESS. CALMNESS AND SMOOTHNESS OF TRANSITIONS.	6			Better
	X	WORKING TROT SITTING					
12	MXK	LENGTHEN STRIDE IN TROT RISING	STRAIGHTNESS. QUALITY OF LENGTHENED TROT AND OF TRANSITIONS.	4	2		Broke
	K	WORKING TROT SITTING					
13	A	DOWN CENTER LINE	STRAIGHTNESS ON CENTER LINE. QUALITY OF HALT.	6			Head came up
	X	HALT. SALUTE.					

LEAVE ARENA AT FREE WALK ON LONG REIN AT A.

COLLECTIVE MARKS:

Gaits (freedom and regularity)	5	2	walk short
Impulsion (desire to move forward, elasticity of the steps, relaxation of the back)	5	2	needs engagement
Submission (attention and confidence; harmony and lightness and ease of movements; acceptance of the bit)	5	2	above bit some
Rider's position and seat; correctness and effect of the aids	6	2	

FURTHER REMARKS:

Ride the horse, not just the test.

50.83 %

SUBTOTAL _122_

ERRORS (-___)

TOTAL POINTS _122_

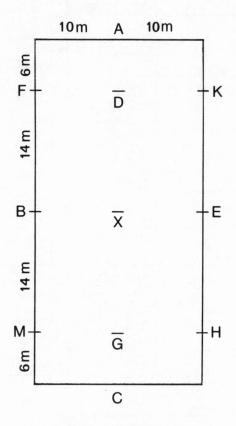

SMALL ARENA
20 x 40 meters

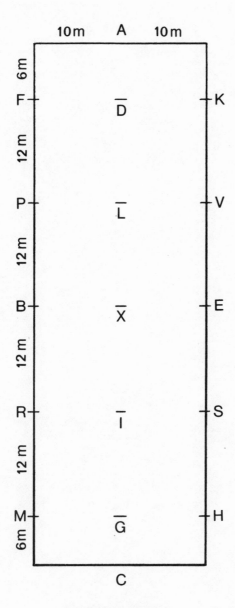

LARGE ARENA
20 x 60 meters